Writing Strategies for U.S. History Classes

A Guide for Teachers

Scott Whipple

Rowman & Littlefield Education
Lanham, Maryland • Toronto • Oxford
2006

Published in the United States of America
by Rowman & Littlefield Education
A Division of Rowman & Littlefield Publishers, Inc.
A wholly owned subsidary of The Rowman & Littlefield Publishing Group, Inc.
4501 Forbes Boulevard, Suite 200, Lanham, Maryland 20706
www.rowmaneducation.com

PO Box 317
Oxford
OX2 9RU, UK

British Library Cataloguing in Publication Information Available

Library of Congress Cataloging-in-Publication Data

Whipple, Scott, 1970–
Writing strategies for U.S. history classes : a guide for teachers / Scott Whipple.
    p. cm.
ISBN-13: 978-1-57886-466-9 (hardcover : alk. paper)
ISBN-10: 1-57886-466-6 (hardcover : alk. paper)
ISBN-13: 978-1-57886-467-6 (pbk. : alk. paper)
ISBN-10: 1-57886-467-4 (pbk. : alk. paper)
1. United States--History--Study and teaching (Secondary) 2. United States—
History—Study and teaching (Secondary)—Activity programs. 3.
Historiography—Study and teaching (Secondary)—United States. 4. United
States—Historiography. I. Title: Writing strategies for United States history
classes. II. Title. E175.8.W48 2006
 973.071—dc22

                                        2006007353

♾️™ The paper used in this publication meets the minimum requirements of
American National Standard for Information Sciences—Permanence of
Paper for Printed Library Materials, ANSI/NISO Z39.48-1992.
Manufactured in the United States of America.

Contents

Introduction

Writing across the curriculum is an excellent tool to reaffirm knowledge of U.S. history, and to encourage the practice of quality writing. The goal of this book is to provide teachers with countless opportunities in which to incorporate a variety of writing methods in their classroom. The strategies suggested range through all types of writing (listed alphabetically), and provide short-term (opening and closing activities) and long-term (semester projects) writing tasks. In addition, this guide contains a unit-by-unit plan with multiple writing activities for each unit.

There are several ways to use this book effectively. You could first browse the list of strategies as they appear in alphabetical order to provide a quick look at the various strategies. Each strategy listed coincides with the main portion of the book, containing a thorough explanation of each mode. For each strategy, three main areas are featured:

- A definition of the strategy.
- An explanation including suggestions as to how to implement the strategy, all of which have been successful in my classroom.
- Topic suggestions for the strategy.

In some cases, the term *unlimited* is used, meaning the number of topics that can be featured is endless.

A second way to use this guidebook is to follow the unit-by-unit planner and assign some or all of the various writing pieces that fit in to the unit being studied in the classroom. This provides an excellent array of alternative assignments to reinforce any reading being done during the unit of study.

A third way to use this book is to determine the amount of time that students will have for a writing task. Do you want the writing to be an opening or closing activity, an in-class writing task, a homework task, or a long-term writing piece? After deciding the answer, refer to the section with strategies categorized by suggested time. When an activity has been selected, refer to the explanation of that activity.

The final way to use this book is to allow for students to take some ownership in their writing. Provide them with a suggested list of writing options to choose from, have them select their writing strategy, and then refer them to the guidebook for proper writing instructions.

Activity Lists

An alphabetical listing of writing activities that can be used in a U.S. history classroom.

adventure story	captions	definitions
advertisement	case studies	descriptions
advice column	chants	diagrams
analysis	cheers	dialogues
announcement	children's books	diaries
antonyms	chronicles	digests
aphorisms	class booklets	directions
argumentation	class anthologies	doggerel
autobiography	classified ads	dramatizations
banners/billboards	comedy monologues	editorials
biographies	comic strips/books	encyclopedia articles
blurbs	commercials	epics
books	comparison essays	epitaphs
book jackets	contrast essays	essays
book reports	conversations	evaluations
brochures	correspondences	explanations
bumper stickers	criticism	eyewitness accounts
business letters	crossword puzzles	fables
calendars	debates	fairy tales

family trees	logs	plaques
feature articles	magazines	plays
fiction	manuals	playbills
fiction diaries	maps	pledges
fliers	matchbook covers	poems
folk tales	memoirs	point of views
forms	memory writings	policies
free-writes	messages	preambles
future predictions	monologues	predictions
generalizations	movie reviews	press conferences
gossip columns	myths	press releases
greeting cards	names	profiles
guided tours	narrations	prophecies
handbills	nature studies	questions
headlines	newsletters	questionnaires
histories	newspapers	quips
historical reporting	news stories	rain checks
historical fiction	notes	recommendations
human-interest stories	notices	renditions
humor column	novels	retrospects
idioms	novelettes	revisions
images	obituaries	riddles
imaginative writings	opinions	road signs
impromptus	ordinances	rule of thumb
instructions	package contents	rumors
interior monologues	pamphlets	salutes
interviews	paragraphs	sanctions
introductions	paraphrase	sarcasms
invitations	partisan opinions	satires
job applications	patent rights	schedules
journals	personifications	script
junk mail	persuasions	self-images
leaflets	petitions	serenades
lectures	philosophies	short story
letters	photo captions	skits
letters to editor	picket signs	slogans
lists	placards	soliloquy

songs	summations	ultimatums
sonnets	surveys	vanity plates
statue plaque	synonyms	warranties
stereotypes	telegrams	welcome
strategies	testimonies	wills
subpoenas	timelines	witticisms

When to Use the Activities

Implementation of innovative writing activities can be done throughout the normal teaching routine of a U.S. history class. The following section provides some ideas as to when to use the various writing activities.

OPENING AND CLOSING ACTIVITIES

Each of the following modes are excellent for opening and closing class time. Each can be modified into a longer writing task.

advertisement	definitions	impromptus
announcements	diagrams	instructions
antonyms	doggerel	interior monologues
aphorisms	epitaphs	introductions
banners/billboards	fliers	invitations
blurbs	free-writes	journals
book jackets	future predictions	leaflets
bumper stickers	generalizations	lectures (1-min.)
captions	greeting cards	lists
chants	headlines	logs
cheers	idioms	matchbook covers
classified ads	images	memoirs
commercials	imaginative writings	memory writings

messages/memos
monologues
names
narrations
notes
notices
obituaries
ordinances
package contents
paragraphs
paraphrase
personifications
persuasions
photo captions
picket signs
placards
plaques
pledges
poems
point of views

preambles
predictions
questions
quips
rain checks
recommendations
renditions
retrospects
revisions
riddles
road signs
rules of thumb
rumors
salutes
sanctions
sarcasms
satires
schedules
scripts
self-images

serenades
slogans
soliloquies
songs
sonnets
statue plaques
stereotypes
strategies
subpoenas
summations
surveys
synonyms
telegrams
ultimatums
vanity plates
warranties
welcome
witticisms

IN-CLASS WRITING ACTIVITIES

With appropriate time variations, each of the following modes may be implemented as an in-class writing assignment.

adventure stories
advertisements
advice columns
analysis
announcements
antonyms
aphorisms
argumentation
autobiographies
banners/billboards

biographies
blurbs
books
book jackets
book reports
brochures
bumper stickers
business letters
calendars
captions

case studies
chants
cheers
children's books
chronicles
class booklets
class anthologies
classified ads
comedy monologues
comic strips/books

commercials
comparison essays
contrast essays
conversations
correspondences
criticism
crossword puzzles
debates
definitions
descriptions
diagrams
dialogues
diaries
digests
directions
doggerel
dramatizations
editorials
encyclopedia articles
epics
epitaphs
essays
evaluations
explanations
eyewitness accounts
fables
fairy tales
family trees
feature articles
fiction
fiction diaries
fliers
folk tales
forms
free-writes
future predictions
generalizations

gossip columns
greeting cards
guided tours
handbills
headlines
histories
historical fiction
historical reporting
human-interest stories
humor columns
idioms
images
imaginative writings
impromptus
instructions
interior monologues
interviews
introductions
invitations
job applications
journals
junk mail
leaflets
lectures
letters
letters to editor
lists
logs
magazines
manuals
maps
matchbook covers
memoirs
memory writings
messages
monologues
movie reviews

myths
names
narrations
nature studies
newsletters
newspapers
news stories
notes
notices
novel
novelette
obituaries
opinions
ordinances
package contents
pamphlets
paragraphs
paraphrasing
partisan opinions
patent rights
personifications
persuasions
petitions
philosophies
photo captions
picket signs
placards
plaques
plays
playbills
pledges
poems
points of view
policies
preambles
predictions
press conferences

press releases
profiles
prophecies
questions
questionnaires
quips
rain checks
recommendations
renditions
retrospects
revisions
riddles
road signs
rules of thumb
rumors

salutes
sanctions
sarcasms
satires
schedules
script
self-images
serenades
short story
skits
slogans
soliloquys
songs
sonnets
statue plaques

stereotypes
strategies
subpoenas
summations
surveys
synonyms
telegrams
testimonies
timelines
ultimatums
vanity plates
warranties
welcome
wills
witticisms

HOMEWORK ASSIGNMENTS

Each of the following activities can be presented as a homework assignment.

adventure stories
advertisements
advice columns
analysis
announcements
antonyms
aphorisms
argumentation
autobiographies
banners/billboards
biographies
blurbs
books
book jackets
book reports
brochures

bumper stickers
business letters
calendars
captions
case studies
chants
cheers
children's books
chronicles
class booklets
class anthologies
classified ads
comedy monologues
comic strips/books
commercials
comparison essays

contrast essays
conversations
correspondence
criticism
crossword puzzles
debates
definitions
descriptions
diagrams
dialogues
diaries
digests
directions
doggerel
dramatizations
editorials

encyclopedia articles
epics
epitaphs
essays
evaluations
explanations
eyewitness accounts
fables
fairy tales
family trees
feature articles
fiction
fiction diaries
fliers
folk tales
forms
free-writes
future predictions
generalizations
gossip columns
greeting cards
guided tours
handbills
headlines
histories
historical reporting
historical fiction
human-interest stories
humor columns
idioms
images
imaginative writings
impromptus
instructions
interior monologues
interviews
introductions

invitations
job applications
journals
junk mail
leaflets
lectures
letters
letters to editor
lists
logs
magazines
manuals
maps
matchbook covers
memoirs
memory writings
messages/memos
monologues
movie reviews
myths
names
narrations
nature studies
newsletters
newspapers
news stories
notes
notices
novels
novelettes
obituaries
opinions
ordinances
package contents
pamphlets
paragraphs
paraphrase

partisan opinions
patent rights
personifications
persuasions
petitions
philosophies
photo captions
picket signs
placards
plaques
plays
playbills
pledges
poems
points of view
policies
preambles
predictions
press conferences
press releases
profiles
prophecies
questions
questionnaires
quips
rain checks
recommendations
renditions
retrospects
revisions
riddles
road signs
rules of thumb
rumors
salutes
sanctions
sarcasms

satires
schedules
script
self-images
serenades
short stories
skits
slogans
soliloquys

songs
sonnets
statue plaque
stereotypes
strategies
subpoenas
summations
surveys
synonyms

telegrams
testimonies
timelines
ultimatums
vanity plates
warranties
welcome
wills
witticisms

UNIT PROJECTS

Each of the following writing strategies provides an excellent opportunity for a unit-ending writing assignment. Each can also be modified into a shorter task.

adventure stories
advice columns
analysis
announcements
antonyms
aphorisms
autobiographies
biographies
books
book jackets
book reports
brochures
business letters
calendars
captions
case studies
chants
children's books
chronicles
class booklets

class anthologies
comic strips/books
commercials
comparison essays
contrast essays
conversations
correspondences
crossword puzzles
debates
diagrams
dialogues
diaries
digests dramatizations
editorials
encyclopedia articles
epitaphs
essays
evaluations
fables
fairy tales

family trees
feature articles
fiction
folk tales
future predictions
generalizations
gossip columns
handbills
headlines
histories
historical fiction
historical reporting
human-interest stories
imaginative writings
impromptus
interviews
job applications
journals
lectures
letters

letters to editor	pamphlets	retrospects
lists	paragraphs	rules of thumb
logs	paraphrase	schedules
magazines	partisan opinions	scripts
maps	persuasions	self-images
memory writings	petitions	short stories
monologues	philosophies	skits
movie reviews	plays	songs
myths	playbills	stereotypes
narrations	poems	strategies
newsletters	points of view	summations
newspapers	predictions	surveys
news stories	press conferences	timelines
novels	press releases	vanity plates
novelettes	profiles	warranties
obituaries	questions	wills
opinions	questionnaire	
ordinances	rain checks	

SEMESTER PROJECTS

Each of the following modes provides an excellent opportunity for a semester project. Each can be modified into a shorter task.

adventure stories	diaries	historical fiction
autobiographies	digests	historical reporting
biographies	dramatizations	human-interest stories
books	editorials	imaginative writings
calendars	epics	impromptus
class booklets	essays	interviews
class anthologies	feature articles	journals
comic strips/books	fiction	lectures
comparison essays	fiction diaries	letters to editor
contrast essays	folk tales	magazines
crossword puzzles	future predictions	manuals
debates	guided tours	maps

memoirs
memory writings
movie reviews
nature studies
newsletters
newspapers
novel
novelette
obituaries
pamphlets
partisan opinions
personifications

persuasions
philosophies
plays
poems
predictions
press conferences
press releases
profiles
prophecies
rain checks
recommendations
renditions

satires
schedules
scripts
skits
songs
sonnets
testimonies
timelines
ultimatums
wills

3

U.S. History Thematic Units

For each of the thematic units, a series of writing tasks is presented. Several examples included can be shared with students:

Discovery and Exploration (Beginnings to 1763)
Colonialism, Revolution, and Early Republic (1763–1800)
A Young Nation Matures (1800–1850)
Union: Division and Rebuilding (1850–1880)
The American West (1877–1900)
Industrialism (1877–1914)
Growth of Cities and Immigration (1875–1915)
Progressive Ideals (1870–1914)
A World Power Emerges (1890–1920)
The Roaring '20s (1920–1929)
Great Depression and A New Deal (1929–1941)
World War II (1931–1945)
A Cold War Heats Up! (1945–1960)
The Booming '50s (1946–1963)
JFK and LBJ: The New Frontier and The Great Society (1960–1968)
Civil Rights (1954–1970)
Vietnam Crisis (1954–1975)
Social Change and Protest (1960–1977)

Nixon, Ford, and Carter (1970–1980)
The '80s to the Present (1980–2000)

DISCOVERY AND EXPLORATION (BEGINNINGS–1763)

Vanity Plates: Design a vanity license plate that might appear on a ship sailing for the New World.

Examples: GO4GOLD (Go for Gold); RGOD2U (Our God to You); CRTZRLZ (Cortez Rules); GOT Au (Got Gold).

Bumper Stickers: Write slogans that would appear on a bumper sticker for a ship sailing to the New World.

Examples: God, Gold, Glory; 3 months to the Promised Land. . . . We Hope!; The New World . . . We'll Take It All!; Round = Riches, Flat = . . .

Brochure: Design a brochure for a company trying to find people to be indentured servants. Glorify the "New World," but make sure to include "fine" print on the brochure.

Prediction: Take on the role of a "New World" resident in the year 1600. Write a predictive news story about the future of your territory. Residents can be expanded to include a personification role. Some examples might be the Cumberland Gap, a lookout post in an Aztec fort, or a tree overlooking Massachusetts Bay or Jamestown.

Examples/Student Prompt: A lookout in an Aztec Fort writes. . . He was surrounded by the masses, all following him. He was half man half beast; a glorious site. He glistened in the high afternoon sun, like the jewels of our land. We had never seen anything like him, only heard stories passed on from generation. The God we had heard about was returning, but little did we know he would not bring joy to our people. . . .

Birth Announcement: Announce the birth of the "New World" to the "Old World." What does a traveler have to look forward to if they choose to sail to the "New World"?

Epitaph: Write an epitaph for a dying "New World." What was good about the previous time frame, and can it get any better? This can be written in the form of a poem also.

Unit Project Suggestions: Adventure Story, Historical Fiction Journal, Newsletter, Memoir of a dying "New World."

COLONIALISM, REVOLUTION, AND EARLY REPUBLIC
(1763–1800)

Chants: Write a series of chants that might be heard as soldiers march toward battle during the Revolutionary War. Include chants for both the Redcoats and the Minutemen.

Examples: "If You're Wearing Red, You're as Good as Dead; I don't know but I've been told . . . Redcoats in our homes is gettin' Old; The Redcoats are coming, The Redcoats are coming, Get your ball and musket, the Redcoats are coming."

Editorial: Write an editorial in favor or opposed to revolution. Assume an identity of someone closely involved with the situation and write in the form of historical fiction.

Comic Book: Design and draw a comic book that details a famous story from the American Revolution.

Business Letter (ultimatums): Take on the role of a member of the Sons of Liberty. Write an ultimatum to King George threatening revolution. Hint at three potential actions or threats, based upon actual historical events. Write a response from King George to the Sons of Liberty. This can be assigned as an exchange writing activity in which students work with partners.

Birth Announcement: Announce the birth of the United States to the "Old World." Include vital statistics, early form of government, future predictions.

Example/Prompt: Thomas Jefferson, Ben Franklin, Thomas Paine, and George Washington, the founding fathers, are proud to announce to the world, the birth of their new child . . . the United States of America. She weighs in at a solid thirteen pounds. This new child will grow in the sound principles of liberty, individuality, and will soon have a written plan for her life. That plan will contain . . .

Rendition: Rewrite the Preamble to the Constitution, or the introduction to the Declaration of Independence in language more representative of our era. Rewrites should represent the same idea of the document, but have different language and interpretation. (Example: All men are created equal. . . . Each gender is the same.)

Opinion/Persuasion: Assume you are a member of an organization called "Keep the Colonies British" with the task of squashing an independence movement. Write a persuasive essay in an effort to convince the colonists to remain loyal. Emphasize three major points in an effort to convince the reader to join your movement. Expand upon main points, refraining from just listing as many as possible. Assume you are a member of "The Sons of Liberty" with the task of promoting an independence movement. Write a persuasive essay in an effort to convince nonbelievers that revolution is the *only* option. Emphasize three major points in an effort to convince the reader to join your movement. Expand upon main points, refraining from just listing as many as possible.

A YOUNG NATION MATURES (1800–1850)

Picket Signs: Design a picket sign to be held by Native American tribes protesting outside of the capitol building as Thomas Jefferson announces the Louisiana Purchase.

Examples: We want the French back!; This Land was Our Land, Now it's Your Land, How Unfair!; Jefferson: A man of the people, just not our people!, Give "our" land back to the French!

Journal: Assume you are a member of the Lewis and Clark expedition. Write a daily entry, or expand into a 1-week journal of the excursion. Include information regarding actual events.

Example/Prompt: Today began like any other day, breakfast cooked by campfire, comments about what we might see, and of course General Clark boosting our spirits with a pep talk. We packed up as usual and off we set in our scow. We sensed our days in the scow were numbered, as an enormous mountain band loomed behind each evening's sunset. We have seen very few tribal groups lately, and assume they are off chasing the Great Buffalo.

Correspondence: Take on the role of Lewis or Clark and write a series of correspondence to a family member, or perhaps to President Jefferson.

What major area of emphasis seems most important for the nation, regarding the newly acquired territory?

Example/Prompt: "To the Honorable Thomas Jefferson: Although our journey is far from over, it is imperative I inform you of some issues that must be dealt with concerning our vast new land. Three major areas could put an internal strain on the United States, and they are . . ."

Nature Study: Research the Lewis and Clark expedition through a primary source, and then write a nature study of a specific area along the route. Focus on a body of water, mountainous area, or specific landscape feature. Include a visualization/map of the work.

Newspaper Story: Assume you are in the Supreme Court chambers the day *Marbury vs. Madison* is heard. Write a newspaper article chronicling the case. Focus on the journalistic questions: Who, What, When, Where, and Why. In your article, make some predictions as to how this might influence the future, using the benefit of hindsight.

Personification: Take on the role of the cotton gin. Write an interior monologue about life as a cotton gin. Describe the mechanism as it works, and also describe the scene: people, places, climate, etc.

Example/Prompt: "I have changed the landscape of the South forever. Cotton fields as far as the eye can see; a white glow across the prairies. Without me, the cotton industry would not be the cash crop it is, yet here I sit inside this shed. Only a few slaves to keep me company. I don't get lonely though because they are always, here, feeding me with the sticky pickings from the fields, expecting my wire teeth to transform the fresh picked cotton, from a dirty sticky bundle to the glorious cotton for the textile mills of the north. . . ."

Press Conference: Write a series of questions and answers for a modern-day press conference with Andrew Jackson. Students take on the role of news reporters and the president, and then act out the conference to the class.

Example: Looking back on your presidency, do you have any regrets? Does the spoils system still work today? Which president since 1900 has been most like Andrew Jackson?

Poem: Complete a poem for one of the following topics: Indian Removal Act, Manifest Destiny, Westward Expansion, or The Gold Rush.

Plaque/Epitaph: Design a plaque/epitaph for one of the following areas: Sutter's Mill, The Alamo, End of Oregon Trail, Cherokee Trail.

Example: We mark this spot as the birth of the great state of California. Thousands upon thousands of people came here searching for gold. In January 1848, gold is first discovered here at Sutter's Mill, leading to mass migration to the region. . . .

UNION: DIVISION AND REBUILDING (1850–1880)

Banner: Create banners that would be carried by a specific military group during a wartime event.

Example: Sherman's march to the sea: "Cutting a swath for the Union!"; Union Army at Gettysburg: "Rebels Beware; this is our Turf!"; Confederacy at Ft. Sumter: "The Strike is on, Down with the Union."

Aphorism: Write a series of aphorisms (adages that describe a person), about prominent Civil War characters. Include several examples that are not necessarily people.

Character Sketch: Create a character sketch of a prominent figure, event, or place of the Civil War. Assignments can be done in one of the following forms: Informative Essay, Poem series, Interior Monologue, Monologue.

Greeting Card: Design and write a passage that would appear on a greeting card sent from someone just arriving in the North after traveling on the Underground Railroad.

Example: I finally reached the Promised Land, and now I must seek a new life. I will begin searching today for work. The struggle is worth it, make every effort to plan your journey. . . .

Dialogue: Write a dialogue that would take place between a Union soldier and a Confederate soldier. Dialogue should convey the historical relevance of "brothers fighting brothers," a common occurrence during the Civil War. Include important elements about the setting, such as date, location, past events, and possible future events.

Leaflet: Design a leaflet that would have been distributed during the Reconstruction period. Focus on one of two areas. Carpetbaggers traveling into the South looking for opportunities or planning schemes, or opportunities for former slaves in the North.

Example/Prompt: "Tired of working for no pay? Tired of not getting anywhere? Go North, young man. The world of work awaits you. Cities like New York and Philadelphia are teeming with job opportunities such as. . ."

Statue Plaque: Write an inscription that would appear on a statue honoring a Civil War hero. Include the location of the plaque as part of the inscription, as well as a date.

THE AMERICAN WEST (1877–1900)

Bumper Stickers: Write slogans that would appear on bumper stickers for a Conestoga wagon traveling across the American frontier.

Examples: "California or Oregon . . . Here we come!"; "Gold or Bust, whichever comes first!"; "This wagon stops at all fort sales. We're wagon-training for life!"

Obituary: Take on the role of a Native American and write an obituary for your tribal group. Include information about people, customs, and culture. This should be an opinionated piece, and might include predictions about the culture.

Telegrams: Write a series of telegrams documenting a journey on one of the following "roads." Oregon Trail, Pony Express, California Trail, Mormon Trail. You should include six stops along the way to transmit from. Telegrams should be written in the form that they would be transmitted via the latest technology for the era.

Example: "trn rt 4 frtl lnd trn lft 4 Au." (Turn right for fertile land, turn left for Gold)

Personification: Assume the role of barbwire, a reaper, or a steel plow, and write an autobiographical selection focusing on how "you" have changed the American Frontier. Writing can be done in several different forms, such as poems, witticisms, satire, fantasy, testimony.

Example/Prompt: Twisted, pulled, stretched, drug through the mud, used as a scratching post, that is my life. I keep cattle where they are supposed to be, but they always try me. I bend and stretch some, but rarely do I break. Check out the tufts of hair in my barbs. I have changed the west forever. . .

News Story: Select an important legislative act affecting the American West, and write a news story, including three predictions about how the legislation would forever change the landscape. Laws to choose from: Dawes Act, Homestead Act, Morrill Act.

Myth: Research the cultural characteristics of a Native American group, and then write a myth that would be appropriate for the culture. Focus on a small aspect of the culture to show better detail as it represents the culture.

INDUSTRIALISM (1877–1914)

Riddles: Select an outcome (invention) due to the rise of industrialism and write several riddles that describe the item or event. Expand into a unit project for creative writing.

Advertisement: Write an advertisement for the sale of a product marketed heavily during the industrial age.

Example/prompt: "Throw away the quill and ink. Now you can produce great works. It's the typewriter, coming to an office near you soon. . . ."

Interview: Write the script for an interview in which an invention or product that changed America takes on a "personified" role and can speak. Question the "product" about the current era, and how they see their role in the development of America. What does the future hold for this "person" being interviewed?

Picket: Design slogans that would appear on picket signs encouraging the formation of a labor union, or for one of the famous strikes of the era (Pullman strike, AFL, Homestead strike).

Example: "No more steeling from us, we want a raise!"; "Wobblies Want More!"; "Carnegie, Share Your Wealth!"

Preamble: Write the preamble to a constitution to be written that promotes workers' rights.

Example/prompt: "We the organized miners of West Virginia, working for a common goal amongst all of us in order to. . . ."

Caption: Display photos from the era of Industrialism, and have students write appropriate captions that correspond to photos.

Example/prompt: "To accompany a photo of two young boys standing in front of a spinning machine in a textile factory: Scarred hands from erratic needles; blistered feet from having to work without shoes. But still they come to work . . . 12, 14, 16 hours per day. If not these two, than two others. As long as the immigrants keep coming for the glories America has to offer, they will toil under the disparages of a sweat-shop. . . ."

Manual: After researching how an invention of the era operates, students are to write an operational manual for on-the-job trainees.

Example/prompt: "The Singer Model 34 sewing machine has three basic functions. Each is quite simple to implement. First . . ."

GROWTH OF CITIES AND IMMIGRATION (1875–1915)

Invitation: Write an invitation to the world population inviting them to come to the United States. Include all the positives they will find.

Satirical Invitation: Write an invitation to the world population inviting them to come to the United States. Write the letter from a cynical point of view, including a negative slant on the real immigrant experience.

Example/Prompt: "The American Dream is alive and well, I just can't seem to find it. I left it all behind to come to the extraordinary United States, but it is not so extraordinary. I want to find that dream, the promise of a great life, but so far all I have is . . ."

Welcome: Write a welcome speech to be given to a group of immigrants just arriving in a major U.S. city. Portray that of a political boss, factory owner, or town mayor.

Profile: Research the development of ethnic community growth in the early 20th century, and write a community profile for a specific location. Focus on how the community is both Americanizing and retaining its ethnic heritage.

Eyewitness Account: Write an eyewitness account of an event that took place in the urban landscape of the growing nation.

Newspaper Story: Write a newspaper story about an event specific to a U.S. city.

Letter to Editor: Write a letter to the editor of an urban newspaper criticizing the role of political machines in local politics.

Example/Prompt: "The founding fathers established this wonderful country with the mantra of government by the people, for the people—a creed for true democracy. Well, in this city, government is only by the people, if they follow the lead of the boss. His idea of government revolves around him. Some examples of this are . . ."

Bio-Poem: Write a bio-poem about an invention or cultural trend that helped to change the social and cultural makeup of the United States during this era. Format: a bio-poem is a way to find out about a character, a person you know, or yourself. The following serves as a skeleton guideline for the poem.

Name, Three traits, Related to, Who cares deeply about, Who feels, Who needs, Who gives, Who fears, Who would like to see, Resident of, Name.

Example/Prompt:

Tenement,
Dark Overcrowded Pungent
Closely associated with slave quarters on a ship
Who cares deeply about nothing . . . if the rent is paid
Who feels the walls stretching, and the halls shrinking
Who needs more occupants
Who fears the day of housing codes
Who gives no breaks for newcomers
Resident of U.S. Cities
Tenement

Advertisement: Design and write an advertisement for a leisure-time event that was growing in popularity during the era.

PROGRESSIVE IDEALS (1870–1914)

Recommendations: Discuss two social areas that a 2000–2005 progressive movement would attack, and why?

Essay: List and explain three distinct events/actions from U.S. history (1920–1970) that could be classified as "Born out of a Progressive Mindset."

Pamphlet: Design and create a pamphlet focusing on an area of society that the progressive movement attacked. Include statistics, stories, and photos.

Political Column: Write a news column in the perspective of a muckraker journalist pointing out a problem for society. Focus on being critical of current government actions.

Pledge: Write a pledge of allegiance for a progressive group. Model it after the U.S. "Pledge of Allegiance," including important elements the group stands for.

   Example/Prompt: "I pledge my word of honor to the adherence of the social and cultural ideals embodied by the unity of the Unified Women of the American States. And to the change and promotion of political and social values to make all citizens equal, despite gender. . . ."

Flyers: Write and design a flyer to be posted around the community making the public aware of a problem in society that a progressive agenda would attack.

Riddle: Select a societal problem that a progressive agenda would be critical about. Write a riddle that describes the problem, and exchange with other students to see if they can guess the problem.

A WORLD POWER EMERGES (1890–1920)

Debate: Work with a partner to write the dialogue of a debate regarding the building of the Panama Canal. Conduct research to include enough information to show both the pro and con side of the issue.

Revision: Rewrite the Treaty of Versailles (assume it is 1920). Address some of the problems that led to WW II as you write the provisions for a treaty to "end all wars."

Editorial: Write a letter to the editor, dateline 1916, supporting war or peace. Make reference to historical events to help strengthen your point.

Telegram: Write a series of telegrams in the form of a timeline covering the duration of the WW I era. Role play a fictional or real person involved in the war.

News Story: Write a news story profiling the causes of World War I or the entrance of the United States into the war.

Example/Prompt: "U.S. Enters War. An allied defeat looked imminent. The United Soviet Socialist Republic was negotiating peace with Germany, and it looked as if Germany would turn its full war machine on France and Great Britain. However, the U.S. has now declared war on Germany. According to President Wilson in his declaration of war speech, the major reasons for U.S. involvement were . . ."

Persuasive Essay: How was World War I preventable? Write a persuasive essay answering the question.

Directions: Write a simple plan of directions for a ship captain that will be driving in a convoy for the first time. Include in your directions how the convoy system works.

Commercial: Write a 30-second commercial script promoting the Selective Service Act of 1917. The intent is to encourage men to sign up for the draft. . . . A patriotic tone should be taken with this.

Example/Prompt: "The U.S. must stop the Germans, and we need your help. Every young American man must answer the call of duty . . . sign up for our team, so you don't end up a part of theirs. Without you, the U.S. won't have enough power. We NEED You!"

Criticism: Write a 30-second commercial script criticizing the Selective Service Act of 1917. The intent is to dissuade men to sign up for the draft. . . . An unpatriotic tone should be taken with this writing selection.

Example/Prompt: "Don't be fooled by President Wilson's propaganda. The U.S. does not need soldiers. You must not sign up for the military it would only cause . . ."

THE ROARING '20S (1920–1929)

News Story: Assume you are a newspaper reporter focusing on the changing workforce of the 1920s. Use three of the following terms to write an article that would be printed in 1924. The terms should all correspond to the topic of the article. *Scientific management, white-collar worker, typing pool, welfare capitalism.*

Definition: Provide two definitions of the 1920s with a one- to three-word theme each. Explain your definition by providing examples to support each theme using common historical terms or terms from the reading.

Comparison Essay or Paragraph: The 1920s and the 1990s are much the same. Provide two common themes that are representative of each decade. Explain each theme, as it is present in each decade.

Letter: Write a series of letters exchanged between one youth living in an urban area and one youth living in a rural area of America during the 1920s. Emphasize a changing lifestyle as Americans moved to the cities.

Dialogue: Create a two- to four-person dialogue using common slang terms of the Roaring '20s (an Internet search should provide adequate lists).

Editorial: Write a letter to a newspaper editor supporting or opposing the passing of the 18th Amendment. Include information regarding cause-and-effect issues based upon historical events.

Additional Assignment: Design a corresponding political cartoon.

Diary: Write a 10-entry diary of a bootlegger. Be as creative as possible.

Slogans: Create a list of prominent people or groups of the '20s (examples: flappers, prohibitionists, bootleggers, isolationists, etc.). For each group, write a slogan that describes their philosophy or political stance. Expand slogans into "campaign statements."

   Example: Flappers: "Coming to a dance party near you"; Prohibitionists: "Liquor, it does a society wrong"; Bootleggers: "Keeping America drinking for 20 years."

Welcome: Write an opening statement welcoming white, middle-class America to the Harlem renaissance. Being serious, or using satire, emphasize the positive cultural impacts that the event will have on America.

THE GREAT DEPRESSION AND A NEW DEAL (1929–1941)

Philosophy Statements: What was the difference in philosophy between Hoover and Roosevelt in their attempts to combat the Depression? What role did each see for the federal government in solving the problem?

Profile: Select one of the groups listed below. Write a cultural profile of that group during the Great Depression. What was their life like? How was it different than the "roaring '20s?" People: urban poor, African Americans, Mexican Americans, farmers, children, women.

Advertisement: Write an advertisement for a farm that is for sale because the owners have moved West. Include satire regarding productivity of farm, compared to the inability to make a profit.

Song/Poem: Write a song or poem celebrating the election of FDR in 1932. Remain positive for Roosevelt, and stay away from criticism of Hoover. Teacher may want to share some examples like, "There's a New Day Coming."

Script: Write a script for an FDR fireside chat. Select a date, and make the address historically accurate.

Example: Dateline 12/24/33. "It is with honor that I speak to you on this holiday evening. Once again I hold the firm belief that the United States is the greatest country in the world, and her citizens are the greatest people in the world. We are still in a time of economic peril, but the future is bright. The programs that are in place are working. The government still has plans to right the ship. Within the next few months we plan to . . ."

Analysis: Explain the significance of the following quote. "The Negro was born in depression. It didn't mean too much to him, The Great American Depression. . . . The best he could be is a janitor or a porter or a shoeshine boy. It only became official when it hit the white man."

Diary/Journal: Bill and Marge graduated form high school in 1930 and married in 1936. Write five entries (quantity can be varied) for either Bill or Marge's diary. Make up one entry for May of 1930, before graduation; the second for September 1935, after the implementation of the New Deal; and the third for January 1937, after their wedding. The other two can be from any timeframe. Have each entry indicate the family problems the person faces at that time, and his or her plans for the future, based upon historical facts.

Essay: Answer the following in a five-paragraph essay: How are the themes, long-term effects of the New Deal, and changing ways of government present in society 60 years after the introduction of the New Deal? This question could be interpreted as vague, so your answer needs to generate a focus (thesis statement) and develop that topic. Make time frame comparisons. Use specific terms and concepts in your answer.

WORLD WAR II (1931–1945)

Headlines/Timeline: Create a WWII timeline by writing a series of appropriate newspaper headlines for 20 events that had a significant impact on World War II.

  Example: "Hitler Forms the Nazis"; "Hitler Pledges Peace in Munich"; "Poland Gets Blitzed, Nazis March On"; "Nazis Invade USSR, Will U.S. Aid?"; "U.S. Has Naval Superiority!"; "A 2nd BOMB!"

Poster: Design a recruitment poster that encourages men and women to volunteer for the armed forces. Include a written and a visual message.

Diary Entry: Imagine that you are a young man or woman who has just learned of the Japanese bombing of Pearl Harbor. You have decided to join the war effort. Write a diary entry that describes your emotions when you learned of the bombing and expresses the reasons for your decision to join up. In the entry, explain what branch of the armed forces you plan to join and whey you chose that branch.

  Example/Prompt: "Well Diary, we are taking a trip. Off to the horizons of Europe with the United States Air Force. I have always been fascinated with flight, and what better way to help my country that to fly planes against the evil Nazis. . . ."

Radio Script: Write a news story to be aired over the radio describing how one of the following could probably lead to WWII. News stories should be predictive in nature. Mussolini's takeover of power in Italy, Hitler's ascent to Chancellor of Germany, Japan's invasion of Manchuria, The United States recognition of the Soviet Union.

  Example/Prompt: "Attention Americans, this just in. Adolph Hitler has been voted Chancellor of Germany. This is sure to lead to world war, it is just a matter of timing. The following reasons are why Hitler's nomination will push the world to war. . . ."

Resume: Create a resume for a world leader at the time of WWII. Resumes should be accompanied with a non-traditional version. Use illustrations, maps, diagrams, symbols, pictures, etc., to document the person, as well as a traditional written resume. Adolph Hitler, Benito Mussolini, Joseph Stalin, Hideki Tojo, Winston Churchill, Franklin Roosevelt.

Informative Essay: You have been asked to advise Roosevelt on war preparations. The date is Dec. 9, 1941. What are three things you would suggest to FDR that need to be done as the U.S. enters WWII, and why would you suggest these?

Handbill: Conduct research on a Broadway production that deals with the WWII era. Write an appropriate handbill for this particular drama, as if it was coming to your school. Include information about topic, historical relevance, characters, and the actors who will portray them (famous or from your school's theater group).

Human Interest/Historical Fiction: Complete an historical fiction piece for someone whose life was greatly impacted by the events of WWII. Conduct research to determine proper accuracy of history, and then fictionalize a character. Selection can be done in the form of diary, correspondence, testimony, retrospect, etc.

A COLD WAR HEATS UP (1945–1960)

Prediction/News Story: Imagine you are a newspaper reporter covering WWII. You have been asked to write an article about the ending of the war. The date is September 1, 1945. Write an article that focuses on three predictions you could make about the future of the world. Base your predictions on historical facts that took place during and after the war.

Editorial Letter: Write a letter to the editor of a newspaper (150 words or less) supporting or criticizing the actions in one of the locations that the U.S. was involved in during the Cold War: Examples: China, Korea, USSR, Vietnam, Hungary, Iran, Egypt.

Example: Refer to student section.

Advertisement: Write an advertisement for a bomb shelter company. Providing a visual prompt of a backyard bomb shelter helps students visualize the image.

Example/Prompt: "What will you do when the big one hits? How will you survive when the Reds attack us with the H-Bomb? Don't get caught in the Cold. This bomb shelter has all the necessities and conveniences to survive a nuclear winter. . . ."

Bio-Poem: Complete a bio-poem for a major aspect of the Cold War. Poems do not have to be about a person, so be creative. Topic ideas might be, but are not limited to, the following: places, events, movements, equipment, etc. (Bio-Poem format on page 23).

Propaganda: Write a statement from the USSR's perspective about the following U.S. actions: Yalta, Potsdam, Atomic bombs, Truman Doctrine, Marshall Plan, NATO, Berlin airlift.

   Example/Prompt: Refer to student section.

Rumor: Select one example of U.S. foreign policy during the Cold War, and describe what you think might have occurred if the U.S. had acted differently. Include outcomes that are far from the truth, but have some historical basis as support.

Sanctions: Write a series of sanctions that the U.S. would impose on a country that is promoting communism. Include social, political, and economic sanctions.

Leaflet: Design a tri-fold leaflet that would be dropped into Berlin during the time of the airlift. Leaflet can be from the perspective of the U.S. or the USSR.

Timeline: Design a timeline that would appear in a news magazine documenting the "History of the Cold War." Include 10–30 events, which cover multiple decades. Expand on entries with summary writings (testimonies, plaques, memoirs).

Debate: Write out dialogue of a debate with the main countries as speakers: U.S. versus USSR and what each country's goals are during the Cold War. Be creative as these two countries come to the brink of war. Include a date that the debate takes place.

THE BOOMING '50S (1946–1953)

Free Write: Select one of the following prompts and complete an 8- to 10-minute free write: How does the pressure to conform affect the American Dream or who might be excluded from the American Dream?

Narrative: "The American Dream was not a reality for every American in the 1950s." Write a first-person narrative supporting this statement using three examples from the time period.

Poem: Write a poem about a cultural phenomenon of the 1950s. Poems can be free verse, or in the bio-poem format. Topics might include: popular food items, TV changing the culture, suburbia, America hits the highway.

Example/Prompt:

Tuna Noodle Casserole
Fish, Cheese, Noodles, Soup
Relative of "sweep the kitchen"
Lover of eager mothers
Who needs great quantities?
Who fears resistant tummies?
Who gives meals a home-cooked touch?
Who would like to see its legacy live forever?
Resident of America
Tuna Noodle Casserole

Biography/Autobiography: Complete a biography writing piece about one of the following historical elements of the 1950s: People, Places, Events, Music Groups, Fads, Trends, TV Character, TV Show, Automobile, Dance Craze. Writing piece can be in the form of a personification, comic strip, plaque inscription, stereotype or news column.

Captions: Provide a series of photos from the era to students and have them write appropriate captions for each photo.

Point of View: After having students read or view the "Checkers speech" by Richard Nixon, have them write a reflective piece stating their point of view on his comments.

Interview: Write an interview dialogue with a cultural phenomenon of the 1950s and have their responses be predictive in nature. Explore the potential cultural impact of the topic, based upon historical occurrences.

Example/Prompt: Interview questions for the hula hoop: What makes people like you? What are some other functions you might serve? Do you see this "fad" lasting forever? What does your popularity say about America?

JFK AND LBJ: THE NEW FRONTIER
AND THE GREAT SOCIETY (1960–1968)

Summary: Write a summary of the outcome of one of the Warren Court cases dealing with defendant's rights.

Prediction: Read JFK's inaugural address, and then write a predictive news story about his presidency. Use of historical knowledge will allow for the writer to document real events. Use text from his address to "predict/support" what actually happened.

  Example/Prompt: "On a typical Washington day in January, newly elected President Kennedy took the oath of office, and then set the nation on a New Frontier. While the temperatures dipped well below zero, and the wind swirled, America learned of the new direction for the nation. President John F. Kennedy will point us in a new direction. With an enthusiastic zeal in his voice, the president outlined his plan for the next four years. . . ."

Sarcasm: Write a sarcastic response from the USSR regarding Kennedy's proposed Peace Corps program. What factors would lead the USSR to be opposed to such a program?

  Example/Prompt: "The United States has done it again, trying to buy the world to their capitalistic way of life. President John F. Kennedy and his "Peace Corps" is not about assisting the world, it is about spreading the fool-hearty philosophy of capitalism. Poor, impoverished peasants of the world don't need capitalism; they need the protective nature of our Communistic system. . . ."

Welcome: Take on the role of a third-world country, and write a personification piece welcoming the Peace Corps volunteers to your country. What areas need improvement, and why are you glad the U.S. is coming?

  Example/Prompt: "On behalf of the poor, starving people of our country, I welcome you to our country (insert name). We have been struggling for years, and look forward to the assistance that this program will offer. Our three main area in which we need support are . . ."

Rumors: Research conspiracy theories regarding the JFK assassination and write a rumor piece featuring one of these conspiracies. Try and cast doubt upon the Warren Commission report.

Retrospect: Write a retrospective piece rating the presidencies of Kennedy and Johnson. Which was more successful, and which has a greater legacy?

Policy: The date is December 1, 1963. Assume the role of policy writer for the Secret Service. Write a new series of policies regarding presidential protection, and include an explanation for the change.

Map Description: Highlight a route that the president could travel from the local airport to your high school. Start with street to exit airport from, and end with door at school to enter. Include a brief write-up explaining the following: Name of each street to take (East on 17th) and three potential trouble spots and a precaution. Include one intersection where two route options are available. Name three streets to entirely close and include why.

Rationale: Write an introduction to a Great Society program and provide historical evidence explaining the rationale for the legislation to be passed. Use examples and statistics from history to support the legislation.

Example/Prompt: "President Johnson is proposing landmark legislation focusing on Civil Rights. The statistics from the last 10 presidential elections clearly show why the bill is appropriate. Upon closer examination of the statistics, one can clearly see . . ."

Press Release: Issue a press release reminding the nation of the importance of a Great Society program that is still in operation in 2005. Include some history of the program, and how it is in operation today.

CIVIL RIGHTS (1954–1970)

Free Write: Complete an 8- to 10-minute free write using the following prompts: "At this bus stop, on December 1, 1955 . . ." "The restaurant was half full when the four black men sat down. . . ." Writing can be done from the perspective of person in picture, person outside of picture, or object in picture.

Captions: Display a series of photos from the Civil Rights era and have students write corresponding captions.

Billboards: Create a series of billboard slogans that might have appeared throughout the segregated South. Include those promoting a segregated society, as well as those that were against segregation (although these would not have been seen).

Example/Prompt: Black in Back, Use the Back Stairs, Not 2nd Class Forever.

Imaginative Writings: Write an editorial piece assuming no segregation exists in America. What would that world look like? Use examples that have happened in history and "twist" their reality to make your desegregated world.

Movie Review: Students are to watch a movie, and write a movie review focusing on the historical implications of the movie.

Petitions: Write a series of petitions that Civil Rights workers would circulate as they strived for equality.

Idioms: Create a list of common idioms that describe all aspects of the Civil Rights struggle.

Examples: Segregationist: "On One's High Horse," Nonviolent protest: "Hold One's Horses."

Character sketch: Create a character sketch of a prominent person, event, or place from the Civil Rights era. Assignments can be done in one of the following modes: poem, biography, self-image, fairy tale (imaginative piece on what is being sought).

Comparison: Complete a "Then & Now" feature for *Plessy v. Ferguson* (then) compared to *Brown v. Board of Education* (now).

Example: Political cartoon that is critical of *Plessy*, and a political cartoon that is in favor of *Brown*, or vice versa. Modes might include, but not necessarily be limited to, the following: comic strips, paragraphs, testimonies, political cartoons, poems, or songs.

VIETNAM CRISIS (1954–1975)

Poem: Students are to write a poem about the year 1968. Poems should provide insight on three major issues that gripped the nation during 1968. Poems should represent the cultural feelings in America during 1968 (protest mentality).

Free Write: Describe the Vietnam War from the following perspectives taken on by Americans. Use the name of at least one different person and one key term as you describe each perspective. 1. The war was first a Crusade! 2. The war was then a Challenge! 3. The war was lastly a Burden!

Persuasive Essay: The Vietnam War years had a positive/negative impact on America. Select from positive/negative viewpoint and defend the statement. Discuss three specific examples to support your answer.

Letter: Assume you are serving in Vietnam and write a letter to someone at home. Make the letter as realistic as possible; put yourself in the position of someone that was there. Each letter should contain the following: four places (map locations), two real people, two fictitious people (fellow soldiers as an example), four relevant statistics, and appropriate dates (viewing *Dear America: Letters Home from Vietnam* provides students with a great model of this type of letter).

Example/Prompt: "Dear Mom & Dad, Day 157, almost halfway through my tour. The weather here is just as miserable as the news reports say, hot & humid all day and not much better at night. We've made it a whole week without losing any members of our platoon. Man how that can change quickly. That's 'Nam though! We are getting the feeling that all is calm for awhile, with the Tet New Year just around the corner. . . ."

Description: Describe the inside of a bunker or armored vehicle that soldiers lived in during their tour in Vietnam. Include examples so that all the senses are stimulated.

Package Contents: Assume you are sending a care package to a soldier in Vietnam. Create a contents list with 15 items, and include a brief description why the soldier would need each of the items in the package.

Analysis: Locate a political cartoon from the Vietnam era. Write an analysis of the cartoon focusing on the following: historical background, cartoon meaning, and political ramifications. What is the artist's opinion of the topic? Include source of cartoon.

Cause and Effect: Write a series of cause-and-effect statements for multiple events of the Vietnam era. What was the result of an event's occurrence? Is there significance to the overall war?

Interview: Create a series of interview questions regarding Vietnam, and then find someone in the community and conduct the interview. Summarize the answers and write a human-interest story regarding their feelings about the Vietnam era.

Example/Prompt: What do you think of when you hear the word Vietnam? How did the Vietnam War have an impact on your family? How would you compare America's current military actions to that of Vietnam?

SOCIAL CHANGE AND PROTEST (1960–1970)

Poem: Write a bio-poem about the counterculture of the 1960s.

Editorial Letter: Write an editorial letter focusing on demands and goals of the AIM during the 1960s and 1970s.

Example/Prompt: "200 years of injustice. The American Indian has suffered long enough. It is time now for the American government to make due on their promises. Our movement wants nothing more than to see our people granted respect. How can we get respect you ask? Following our simple plan with these three steps will ensure equality. . . ."

Protest Letter: Write a letter encouraging the boycotting of grapes as promoted by the United Farm Workers Organizing Committee.

Protest Posters: Create a series of protest poster slogans for any of the groups struggling to achieve equality or notoriety during the 1960s.

Dialogue: Create a two- to four-person dialogue between members of the counterculture. Use common language/slang terms from the era. Examples can be found on several different websites.

Editorial Letter: Write an editorial letter for or against the ratification of the Equal Rights Amendment.

NIXON, FORD, AND CARTER (1970–1980)

Subpoena: Write out a subpoena for President Nixon to appear before the people of the United States to answer for potential crimes regarding Watergate.

Example/Prompt: It shall be duly noted that Richard Millhouse Nixon shall appear before the United States people to answer for the crimes detailed in the Watergate investigation. He shall have to answer to any and all questions brought forth by the U.S. Senate Select Committee. "The major elements he shall be questioned on will be . . ."

Memo: Write a series of memos that might have circulated around the White House during the Watergate era. Write memos in which President Nixon is the sender or the recipient.

Example/Prompt: "To: Richard Nixon; From: Gerald Ford: President Nixon, Please take the tape recording machines with you when you go. I won't be here too long, thanks to your blundering, and they might only cause me trouble. Sincerely, G. Ford."

Questionnaire: Write a series of questions to be asked of Richard Nixon 10 years after his leaving office. Create answers that he might have given or exchange with another student and have them write the answers.

Headlines: Create a timeline of Nixon's presidency by writing a series of news headlines that would have appeared.

Press Conference: Write a script that President Carter might read immediately after taking office. Read to class.

Example/Prompt: "I come before the American people tonight with a strong message towards healing. We need to forget the past, and look towards the future now as our administration looks to fix the ills that are upon this great nation. We should not dwell on the past as we have a lot to look forward to. . . ."

Recommendation: President Ford has asked for your recommendation on the question, "Should I pardon Richard Nixon?" Assume the role of a presidential advisor and give him your recommendation.

News Story: Read Jimmy Carter's inaugural address and then write a news story previewing Carter's presidency. What does Carter propose for the nation? How does he intend to improve the nation?

'80S TO THE PRESENT (1980–2005)

Summary: Write a paragraph about Ronald Reagan's major domestic goals using the following terms: Reaganomics, Supply-Side Economics, Deregulation, National-Debt.

Book Jacket: Assume you are writing a book jacket for a book entitled *Reagan's Foreign Policy Victory: Defeating the USSR.* Include the following terms in your chapter previews: Glasnost, Gorbachev, SDI, Berlin Wall, three Prior Presidents.

Poem/Song: Write a short song or poem using the TV influences of 2000–2005 as a basis for content. Writing can be done to a common musical tune or just in poetic format. Include types of shows and common themes emphasized on TV.

Slogans: Create campaign slogans for each candidate during the elections of 1980, 1984, 1988, 1992, 1996, 2000, and 2004.

Example/Prompt: 1980: "I can at least Act like a President." "1984: 4 more Oscars! Vote Reagan."

1996: "Down with the Texan, Bring on the Arkansan!"

Opinion: Write an opinion piece on why the U.S. is the victim of terrorist activity. Emphasize how we have changed from the world's "police," to the world's "target."

4

Activity Descriptions

The following pages contain the strategies in alphabetical order, with accompanying definition, explanation, and topic suggestions.

A

Adventure Story

Definition: An enterprise of a hazardous nature with an exciting experience, or involving risk.

Explanation: Historical fiction opportunity that allows student writers to research, conceptualize, and envision the difficulties experienced by those in history that faced great risk in an effort to achieve a goal. May be written as a 1st person narrative, or in 2nd person.

Topics to Utilize Strategy: Explorers, Pilgrims, Minutemen, Colonists, Underground Railroad, Westward Expansion, Lewis & Clark, Gold Miners, Soldiers, Pilots, Immigrants, Slaves.

Advertisement

Definition: A public announcement; to make known; to warn or notify.

Explanation: 1. Written ad to be read as part of a TV or radio broadcast, making people aware of historical events, or opportunities for their participation.

2. Design a visual ad to make people aware of historical events, or opportunities. Ads should be used for billboards, news banners, or flyers. Visual ads can be used with an accompanying caption or script.

Topics to Utilize Strategy: Colonization, Free land in New World, Indentured Servants, Triangular Trade, Revolution, Minutemen Organizations, Ratification of Constitution, Land in Texas, Gold Rush, Underground Railroad, Land on Frontier, Political Machines, Soldiers for War, Speakeasies, Stocks for Sale (Depression), Concentration Camps, Rosie Riveter, Bomb Shelter Sales, Rock & Roll Concerts, Great Society Programs, Montgomery Bus Boycott, Automobiles, Presidential Campaigns.

Advice Column

Definition: Opinions about a course of action appearing regularly in a newspaper.

Explanation: Individual features providing students an opportunity to express opinions regarding a topic. May be implemented from a historical perspective (Yes, that was a good/bad action), or writers take on the role of someone living during a historical event, and advise citizens or important people.

Topics to Utilize Strategy: Is the World Flat?, Revolution & Independence, Federalist vs. Anti-Federalist, Ratification, Secession, Manifest Destiny, Native American Perspective on Westward Expansion, Labor Union Formation, Yellow Journalism, American Military Action . . . Neutrality or War, Treaties, Atomic Bomb (Written to Truman), Berlin Airlift, Presidential Elections, Star Wars.

Analysis

Definition: The separation of the whole into its parts. Perceptions of the parts and interrelations to the whole.

Explanation: A break down look at smaller components of an action emphasizing the overall impact on the event.

Topics to Utilize Strategy: Individual Battles of a War, Various Areas within the Progressive Movement, Presidential Speech Analysis.

Announcement

Definition: To make known publicly; to proclaim the arrival of.
Explanation: See Advertisement
Topics to Utilize Strategy: Unlimited

Antonyms

Definition: A word meaning the opposite of another word.
Explanation: Allows students to use adjectives and adverbs to describe specific events in history. Utilized like a Rorschach ink blot test. Teacher provides a list of events (orally or written); students provide antonyms for the event (may also be done with synonyms).
This works well as a semester review activity.
Topics to Utilize Strategy: Unlimited.

Aphorisms

Definition: A maxim, or adage (short proverb). A brief statement of a principle.
Explanation: Students are to write aphorisms that speak about specific historical figures or events. *Example*: Franklin: Lost time is never found again.
Topics to Utilize Strategy: Individual Citizens, Movements, Historical Eras.

Argumentation

Definition: The presentation and elaboration of an argument, the discussion of differing opinions.
Explanation: Students write an opinion regarding events or actions in history from the perspective of one or two sides. May be done in the form of a debate, in which students write the dialogue, and then perform the debate/argument.
Topics to Utilize Strategy: Pro or Con: Revolution, Westward Expansion, War, Louisiana Purchase, Presidential Candidates, Labor Union, Immigration Laws, Atomic Warfare, Cold War Politics, Segregation, ERA, Star Wars.

Autobiography

Definition: Biography of a person written by that same person.

Explanation: Students write from the perspective of a specific person in history, or take on the role of an event. This is an excellent opportunity for personification in student writing. Length suggestion: 1-paragraph up to a full paper.

Topics to Utilize Strategy: Important People, Bystanders to a Situation (Witness to Boston Massacre, Witness on Grassy Knoll in Dallas), Objects of Historical Importance (Wagon Trains, Spinning Looms, Equipment Used in Panama, Statue of Liberty, U2 Spy Plane).

B

Banners/Billboards

Definition: A headline spanning the width of a newspaper; a poster recognizing great accomplishment.

Explanation: Used to capture moods or mindsets of groups in history. Teacher instructions should focus students themes for banners for parades, advertisements, or protests.

Topics to Utilize Strategy: Explorers' Ships, Redcoat Supporters, King George Support, Colonization Supporters, Alamo Sign, Underground Railroad, Versailles Treaty, Muckraker Topics, New Deal Supporters, Presidential Candidates, American Dream, Automobile Culture, Court Cases, Roads & Byways (Route 66, Ho Chi Minh Trail).

Biographies

Definition: An account of a person's life written or produced by someone else.

Explanation: Students write about a specific person or event in history. Directing students to complete a biography about an event or object, as opposed to a person, broadens their understanding of the event. An interesting twist to this assignment is for students to write a biography of a person that has not had one written before. An example would be a grandparent.

Topics to Utilize Strategy: Important People, Objects of Historical Importance (Wagon Trains, Spinning Looms, Equipment Used in Panama, Statue of Liberty, U2 Spy Plane), Movements (Colonization, Independence, Revolution, Progressives, Civil Rights, Gold Rush, Westward Migration, Cold War, Counterculture).

Blurbs

Definition: A brief favorable publicity notice, as on a book jacket.

Explanation: Short sentences or phrases praising the actions of historical figures. Instruct students that they are to write the publicity for an upcoming release regarding a historical figure or event: perhaps even the publicity for a biography.

Topics to Utilize Strategy: Unlimited.

Books

Definition: Printed or written literary work.

Explanation: May be utilized as a class project. Groups of students can be assigned a chapter focusing on historical figures, movements, or eras. Books can be biography, informative, critical expose, etc. Use caution with regard to plagiarism.

Topics to Utilize Strategy: Unlimited.

Book Jackets

Definition: Highlight/publicity for a book; short recognition of the author.

Explanation: Short sentences or phrases praising the author or the content. Instruct students that they are to write the publicity for an upcoming release regarding a historical figure or event.

Topics to Utilize Strategy: Unlimited.

Book Reports

Definition: A formal and detailed account of a book.

Explanation: Formal analysis of books. Specific guidelines help students to focus on the topic. Encourage students to steer away from just plot summary, and focus on the historical ramifications—especially if the book is the genre of historical fiction.

Topics to Utilize Strategy: Biography, Autobiography, Classic Literature, Nonfiction, Historical Fiction.

Brochures

Definition: A pamphlet often containing promotional material.

Explanation: Assign tri-fold brochures to coincide with technology-related curriculum. Programs like *Microsoft Publisher* allow for students to explore the areas of technology. Use caution with regard to plagiarism.

Topics to Utilize Strategy: Travel Destinations, Specific States, Specific Decades, Historical Sites, Tourist Locales, Battlefields, Historical Eras.

Bumper Stickers

Definition: Short phrases usually containing irony or witty remarks.

Explanation: A great method to teach students to be critical and analytical of historical actions and events. Require students to present a bumper sticker in favor of the party that does not benefit from historical actions/events.

Topics to Utilize Strategy: Design bumper stickers for the following: Columbus's Ships, Cortez Ship, Pilgrims' Ships, British Vessels, Paul Revere's Horse, Slave Ships, Erie Canal Vessels, Wagon Trains, Military Convoys to the Great Plains, Underground Railroad "Cars," Custer's Horse, Immigrant Ships, Steam Shovels in Panama, Warships (Various Eras), Model T, Lindbergh Plane, Great Migration Travelers, Bonus Army Vehicle, Berlin Airlift Airplane, U2 Spy Plane, Freedom Riders Bus, Montgomery Bus Boycott Car, Bike along the Ho Chi Minh Trail, B-52, Nuclear Warhead.

Business Letters

Definition: A professional, formal manner of communication.

Explanation: Students are to write formal letters to historical figures, supporting, opposing, and questioning actions. This can also be assigned as a role-play letter in which the student takes on the role of a famous figure and writes a letter to a recipient.

Topics to Utilize Strategy: World Leader to World Leader, President to U.S. Citizen, President to War Hero, President to Family Member of Soldier, etc., Citizen to Historical Figure.

C

Calendars

Definition: Various systems of recognizing the months and days of the year.

Explanation: Students will design and document events during a specified time period, similar to a timeline. Calendars can be split into weeks, months, or years, with the level of depth dependant upon length of time. Use caution with regard to plagiarism.

Topics to Utilize Strategy: Cuban Missile Crisis, Berlin Airlift, U.S. Involvement in World War, Watergate Activity, New Deal Activity, Civil Rights Time Frame, Montgomery Bus Boycott.

Captions

Definition: A short legend or description accompanying an illustration; a title of a document or article.

Explanation: An excellent activity to challenge minds to think. Display photos on overhead or pass a series of photos around room, requiring each student to write an appropriate caption. After writing, have students read, or listen to others, which provides a variety of ideas to be shared and absorbed by each student. An excellent opening or closing activity. This can be expanded into a task in which the students research photos, and write appropriate captions. Some prompts for caption writing include: 1. Person in picture (PIP), first person from the perspective of someone in photo; 2. Object in picture (OIP), first person from the perspective of an object in photo; 3. Person outside of picture (POP), witness to a photo. An interesting twist on this strategy is to require the students to research a photo, download it along with the source, and then do the writing assignment.

Topics to Utilize Strategy: Unlimited.

Case Studies

Definition: A detailed analysis of a person or group; especially as a model of medical, psychiatric, or social phenomena.

Explanation: This becomes a biography of a cultural group or subgroup. When assigned in class, students need to be cautioned regarding stereotypes and bias. This works well for exploration into the "other side" of an argument or historical situation.

Topics to Utilize Strategy: Individual Historical Figures, Cultural Groups, Incas, Aztecs, Mayans, New England, Middle Colonies, Southern Colonies, Red Coats, Patriots, Native American Groups, Soldiers, Unionists, Confederates, American Melting Pot, Immigrants, Muckrakers, Okies, Communists, Poor America, Conservatives, Liberals.

Chants

Definition: A series of syllables sung on the same note; to sing a chant.

Explanation: Inspirational bits of singing to rally a group of supporters. Can be utilized to emphasize beliefs of a particular cultural group. Students should write and perform chants so that others can determine who or what they are supporting. Students can write a rallying cry for a group struggling for a cause.

Topics to Utilize Strategy: Colonists, Federalists/antiFederalists, Westward Expansionists, Slaves, Secessionists, Native Americans, Labor Unions, Progressives, Imperialists, Communists, Red Scare Proponents, New Dealers, Bonus Army, American Poor, Civil rights, Hawks/Doves.

Cheers

Definition: A shout of encouragement or congratulation.

Explanation: A poetic or lyrical series of chants showing support for a cause. Can be utilized to emphasize beliefs of a particular cultural group. Students should write and perform cheers so that others can determine who or what they are supporting. Students can write a rallying cry (cheer) for a group struggling for a cause.

Topics to Utilize Strategy: Colonists, Federalists/antiFederalists, Westward Expansionists, Slaves, Secessionists, Native Americans, Labor Unions,

Progressives, Imperialists, Communists, Red Scare Proponents, New Dealers, Bonus Army, American Poor, Civil Rights, Hawks/Doves.

Children's Books

Definition: Books designed for younger ages, usually with accompanying photos.

Explanation: Students should design, write, and illustrate a book intended for children. Topics should be specific, with vocabulary being age appropriate. This would be an excellent opportunity to partner with an elementary school for cross-age learning, service project.

Topics to Utilize Strategy: Unlimited, but should be specific (D-Day) rather than general (WWII).

Chronicles

Definition: An account of historical events arranged in order of their occurrence.

Explanation: A written description of a timeline. Sometimes an accompaniment to a timeline. Suggestion for better writing success is to require that the number of time line entries be more than the number of entries chronicled. For example: Timeline with 20 dates documented, and 6 chronicled . . . depending on time allowed.

Topics to Utilize Strategy: Unlimited.

Class Anthologies

Definition: A collection of selected writings organized by topic or theme.

Explanation: Great to use as a unit or semester review. Assign each group or individual a specific area for their writing. Collect information, and organize into a booklet. Share with class whenever possible. This works well to post to a website and then require students to read and write some type of review on the entire booklet. Anthologies can be assigned using a specific strategy, a specific topic, or both.

Topics to Utilize Strategy: Unlimited.

Class Booklets

Definition: A series of topics organized into a formal book or packet.

Explanation: Great to use as a unit or semester review. Assign each group a specific area to become experts about, collect their information in a specified form, with specific requirements, and organize into a booklet. Share booklets with class. This works well to post to a website, and then require students to read and write some type of review on the entire booklet.

Topics to Utilize Strategy: Unit topics or class themes.

Classified Ads

Definition: A brief ad in a newspaper or magazine with others of the same kind.

Explanation: Designed to make students aware of the cultural environment and setting of specific historical eras. Students can formulate ads for different people in different eras. Ads can also be included in a class newspaper activity.

Topics to Utilize Strategy: Unlimited.

Comedy Monologues

Definition: A humorous speech by one person often monopolizing a conversation.

Explanation: Students take on the role of a historical figure and provide a monologue with intended sarcasm and wit regarding a situation. Monologues should contain irony, noting a sense of disapproval from the speaker. This also works well for students to take on a role of personification of an event, movement, or item of relevance.

Topics to Utilize Strategy: People: Presidents, Muckrakers, Native Americans, Imaginary Political Assistants, Soldiers, Foreign Leaders.

Personifications: Sailing Vessels, Land Marks, Mineshafts, War Ordinance, Presidential Symbols (Big Stick), Political Machines, Nuclear Weaponry, Aircraft, Booby Traps (Vietnam War), Satellites.

Comic Strips/Books

Definition: A series of cartoon strips organized into a book.

Explanation: This allows for student creativity and artistic expression to come out with regard to specific topics. May be combined with the children story strategy. Emphasis may sometimes be placed on artwork and creativity.

Topics to Utilize Strategy: Specific events in history work well.

Examples: Columbus to America, Pilgrim Story, Boston Tea Party, Boston Massacre, Paul Revere's Ride, Lewis & Clark, Underground Railroad, Civil War Battles (Brothers Fighting Brothers), Wounded Knee, Wright Brothers, Roaring '20s and Flappers, Okie Migration, WWII Battles, Red Scare, Montgomery Bus Boycott, Kent State.

Commercials (see Advertisements)

Definition: An advertisement for television or radio.

Explanation:

Topics to Utilize Strategy: See Advertisement.

Comparison Essays

Definition: A short literary composition noting the similarities of two or more items.

Explanation: An essay comparing two similar events or people in history. May be combined with a comparison/contrast essay.

Topics to Utilize Strategy: Unlimited.

Contrast Essays

Definition: A short literary composition noting the differences of two or more items.

Explanation: An essay contrasting two events in history. May be combined with a comparison/contrast essay.

Topics to Utilize Strategy: Unlimited.

Conversations

Definition: An exchange of dialogue between people, objects, or subjects.

Explanation: Allows for students to reenact important events in history. May be implemented into a monologue in which a historical figure discusses events with an object in his presence (bombardier talking to the first atomic bomb moments before dropping).

Topics to Utilize Strategy: Unlimited.

Correspondences

Definition: Communication by the exchange of letters.

Explanation: Student to student role-plays in which students role-play characters and exchange letters. Can also be utilized by instructors reading a letter to the entire class, and they each write a response directed at the teacher (historical figure).

Topics to Utilize Strategy: (each can be reversed for effect) Colonist to Englishman, Colonist to King George, Jefferson to Paine, President to Opponent, President to Foreign Leader, Jefferson to Lewis & Clark, Wagoneer to Parents, Immigrant to Homeland (Parents), Former Slave in North to Slave in South, Native American to U.S. President, Jim Crow to Anyone, Panamanian to Roosevelt, Dead Soldier's Parents to President, Soldiers Letter Home (works especially well after viewing *Dear America, Letters Home from Vietnam* or similar documentary films), FDR to Hoover, Marshall to the World (after plan), President to Former President.

Criticism

Definition: A comment or judgment marked by careful evaluation.

Explanation: Individual features providing students an opportunity to express opinions regarding a topic of history. May be implemented from historical perspective (Yes, that was a good/bad action), or writers take on the role of someone living during a historical event, and advise citizens or important people.

Topics to Utilize Strategy: Is the World Flat?, Revolution/Independence, Federalist vs. Anti-Federalist, Ratification, Secession, Manifest

Destiny, Native American Perspective on Westward Expansion, Labor Union Formation, Yellow Journalism, American Military Action . . . Neutrality or War, Treaties, Atomic Bomb (written to Truman), Berlin Airlift, Presidential Elections, Star Wars.

Crossword Puzzles

Definition: A puzzle consisting of numbered squares to be filled with answers to clues.

Explanation: Excellent review activity requiring students to describe events and people from areas of study. Emphasis should be placed on clues being unique, and not just word-for-word copy from textbooks.

Topics to Utilize Strategy: Unlimited.

D

Debates

Definition: A formal contest of argumentation in which two opposing ideas are deliberated.

Explanation: Students write scripts for a debate.

Topics to Utilize Strategy: Unlimited.

Definitions

Definition: A statement of the meaning of a word, phrase, or term.

Explanation: Excellent way to improve vocabulary of students. Emphasis needs to be placed on definitions being written in own words, not copied form textbook. Excellent pre- or post-unit activity.

Topics to Utilize Strategy: Unlimited.

Descriptions

Definition: A verbal account of.

Explanation: Students role-play from the perspective of a first-hand witness, and retell their story. Writing tends to be richer if students are given a prompt. (I will remember December 7, 1941 like it was yesterday. It was a bit overcast when I first heard the planes. . . .)

Topics to Utilize Strategy: Unlimited, but should focus writing to a specific event.

Diagrams

Definition: A schematic plan or drawing designed to explain how something works or to clarify the relationship between the parts of a whole.

Explanation: Students describe a drawing or plan to emphasize the visual and written understanding of an event/action. The focus is on multiple learning styles. One method is to have students design a map, and then provide a description of all items included.

Topics to Utilize Strategy: Assembly Line, Cotton Gin, Slave Ship Diagram, Middle Passage, Explorer Route, Alamo Layout, Gettysburg Battle Description, Rail Route, Ho Chi Minh Trail, Shifting Frontier, Canal System, Dealey Plaza.

Dialogues (see Conversations)

Definition: Conversation between two or more people.

Topics to Utilize Strategy: See Conversations.

Diaries

Definition: A daily record of personal experiences and observations. A daily journal.

Explanation: Students write from the perspective of a specific person in history or take on the role of an event. This is an excellent opportunity for personification in student writing. Length suggestion: one-paragraph up to a full paper (similar to autobiography, but focus can be on one day's events).

Topics to Utilize Strategy: Important People, Bystanders to a Situation (Witness to Boston Massacre, Witness on Grassy Knoll in Dallas), Objects of Historical Importance (Wagon Trains, Spinning Looms, Equipment Used in Panama, Statue of Liberty, U2 Spy Plane).

Digests (see Class Booklets)

Definition: A collection of written material in condensed form.
Explanation:
Topics to Utilize Strategy: Unlimited.

Directions

Definition: An instruction or series of instructions for doing or finding something.
Explanation: A task designed to emphasize the geography of a historical place. Students should focus on important landmarks as they provide details in their directions.
Topics to Utilize Strategy: Unlimited.

Doggerel

Definition: Clumsy verse often irregular in form and humorous in effect.
Explanation: Short passages intended to provide wit or humor toward an event or action of history. Generally critical in nature, wit and irony are emphasized.
Topics to Utilize Strategy: Presidential Action, Presidential Folly, Legislation, Fallen Heroes.

Dramatizations

Definition: To present or view in a dramatic or melodramatic way; prose or verse composition especially for performance.
Explanation: Scene writing that can be performed to emphasize the importance of historical events.
Topics to Utilize Strategy: Unlimited.

E

Editorials

Definition: An article expressing the opinion of its editors or publishers.

Explanation: Individual features providing students an opportunity to express opinions regarding a topic of history. May be implemented from historical perspective (Yes, that was a good/bad action), or writers take on the role of someone living during a historical event, and advise citizens or important people (similar to criticism).

Topics to Utilize Strategy: Is the World Flat?, Revolution and Independence, Federalist vs. Anti-Federalist, Ratification, Secession, Manifest Destiny, Native American Perspective on Westward Expansion, Labor Union Formation, Yellow Journalism, American Military Action . . . Neutrality or War, Treaties, Atomic Bomb (Written to Truman), Berlin Airlift, Presidential Elections, Star Wars.

Encyclopedia Articles

Definition: Individual item in a comprehensive reference work.

Explanation: Caution is necessary to avoid plagiarism.

Topics to Utilize Strategy: Unlimited, but focused.

Epic

Definition: A long narrative poem celebrating the feats of a traditional hero.

Explanation: An excellent alternative to obituary assignments, in which the student highlights the life of the subject in heroic fashion.

Topics to Utilize Strategy: Unlimited in scope. Can be altered to include movements or events, in addition to people. Examples: Civil Rights, Great Depression, World War, Progressivism, etc.

Epitaphs

Definition: An inscription on a tombstone in memory of a deceased person.

Explanation: Provides opportunity for students to show creativity and expanded use of language. Can be altered into poetic tributes. This can be assigned for a specific person, event, or era.
Topics to Utilize Strategy: Unlimited.

Essays

Definition: A short literary composition on a specific subject, presenting the personal view of the author.
Explanation:
Topics to Utilize Strategy: Unlimited.

Evaluations

Definition: To analyze or fix the value of; rating of one's performance.
Explanation: Allows for students to rank and provide a basis for determining importance. Which actions were best or which events had more significance throughout history.
Topics to Utilize Strategy: Unlimited.

Explanations

Definition: To make plain or comprehensible; to define or expound.
Explanation: Summary of important points, lectures, or reading selections.
Topics to Utilize Strategy: Unlimited.

Eyewitness Accounts

Definition: Description of a person seeing an event.
Explanation: Students write a role-play from the perspective on an eyewitness, or "eyeobject" (personification of objects). A prompt may be used to focus writing. Example: "I can't believe Rosa Parks would not stand up. . . ."
Topics to Utilize Strategy: Unlimited.

F

Fables

Definition: A fictitious story making a moral point and often using animals as characters; a story about legendary persons and exploits.

Explanation: Creative method in which students explore the rationale of historical events. A fictional writing opportunity implemented to emphasize aspects of history.

Topics to Utilize Strategy: Exploration, Colonization, Native American Legends, Indentured Servants, Pioneers, Underground Railroad Hero, Political Boss, Jim Crow, Bull Moose, Heroic Soldiers.

Fairy Tales

Definition: A fanciful tale of legendary deeds and creatures, usually intended for children.

Explanation: Similar to a children's book, the story is made to be extraordinary for better comprehension of a low-level learner/reader.

Topics to Utilize Strategy: Unlimited.

Family Trees

Definition: A genealogical diagram of a family's ancestry.

Explanation: This can be expanded into designing a family tree of an event or historical era.

Topics to Utilize Strategy: Unlimited.

Feature Articles

Definition: A prominent article or story in a magazine or newspaper.

Explanation: Informative essays on a specific topic. Caution should be used here to avoid plagiarism.

Topics to Utilize Strategy: Unlimited. Man of the Year, Event of the Decade, Battle of the Century, Song of the Year.

Fiction

Definition: A literary work whose content is produced by the imagination and is not based on fact.

Explanation: Utilization of various strategies with a historical fiction angle. Fictitious characters spun into an actual historical event. An excellent first-person writing activity.

Topics to Utilize Strategy: Unlimited.

Fictional Diaries

Definition: A daily record of personal experiences and observtions, or a daily journal whose content is produced by the imagination and not based on fact.

Explanation: Expanded into a historical fiction account . . . Eyewitness writing prompts.

Topics to Utilize Strategy: Unlimited.

Fliers (see Advertisements)

Definition: A circulation for mass distribution.

Topics to Utilize Strategy: See Advertisement.

Folk Tales

Definition: The traditional beliefs, legends, and practices of a people, sometimes passed down orally. Sometimes referred to as folklore.

Explanation: Creative writing opportunity for students to explore the ideology of a specific culture. Written in the form of a story that would be read orally.

Topics to Utilize Strategy: Unlimited, Native American Lore, Cultural Minority Groups.

Forms

Definition: A document with blanks for the insertion of requested information.

Explanation: Similar to a job application, this allows students to prepare a type of survey for information. Forms may be teacher designed for students to complete or forms may be student designed.

Topics to Utilize Strategy: Recruitment of Followers or Soldiers, Underground Railroad Participants, Labor Union Application, Political Machine Information, Hawk/Dove Information, Communist Witch Hunt Forms.

Free-Writes

Definition: Continuous writing for a timed period.

Explanation: Provide students with a prompt to focus writing and encourage them to be creative.

Topics to Utilize Strategy: Unlimited.

Future Predictions

Definition: To state, tell, or make known in advance; to speculate as to future outcomes.

Explanation: Utilizing hindsight as a basis, students make predictions (like in a news story) as to the future, following a major event. "It is September 1, 1945, write a news story making three predictions about the future of the world."

Topics to Utilize Strategy: Unlimited, but students should be focused to a specific event ending. Example: WWII and the apparent beginning of the Cold War.

G

Generalizations

Definition: Broad but not thorough statements; to speak or write vaguely.

Explanation: Activity for pre-unit writing task. Students are to write generalizations about an upcoming unit, making predictions as to what the content might contain. Similar to a KWL reading strategy.
Topics to Utilize Strategy: Unlimited.

Gossip Columns

Definition: Rumor or talk of a personal, sensational, or intimate nature.
Explanation: Creative writing task in which students can use facts from history to speculate on historical figures or events. Allows for speculation regarding events or people; may be used as a prediction writing task.
Topics to Utilize Strategy: Unlimited.

Greeting Cards

Definition: A folded card bearing a message . . . greetings, congratulations, thank you, sorrow.
Explanation: Creative writing task in which students write messages synonymous of a historical situation. Cards can be from one person to another or one place to another or one era to another or one movement to another. This is an excellent strategy to combine a writing and visual assignment by requiring an artistic feature to the card.
Topics to Utilize Strategy: Explorers to Home, New World to Old World, Indentured Servant to Home, Old NW to NE Family Member, Colony Group to Colony Group, Plains Indian to SW Indian, Slave State to Free State, Custer to Family, Soldier to Family.

Guided Tours

Definition: Leading or directing the way through a relevant area, such as a city, place, or movement.
Explanation: A task designed to emphasize the geography of a historical place. Students should focus on important landmarks as they provide details in their directions.
Topics to Utilize Strategy: Unlimited.

H

Handbills

Definition: A printed sheet distributed by hand; a preview of a show or musical performance.

Explanation: Students are provided with a topic for a play or musical performance (usually by instructor) and then they are responsible for writing a handbill for the production. Include actors, scene titles, relevant song titles, etc. For musical selections, students can choose from songs already produced (include proper reference to songwriter/singer) or make up song titles they think would be appropriate.

Topics to Utilize Strategy: Unlimited.

Headlines

Definition: Title or caption of a newspaper article meant to get attention or preview a story.

Explanation: After being given events from history, students write appropriate headlines. A way to review a topic would be to assign students to write 15 headlines that might appear on a newspaper for a given day. Headlines should encompass the entire scope of the culture. Options: Students can write headlines and then exchange with others to research the dates of events.

Topics to Utilize Strategy: Unlimited.

Histories

Definition: The events of the past, a culminating story.

Explanation: Review activity for events, actions, people, or movements. This works well by combining one of the strategies and incorporating into a history: Letter to Editor, Song, Riddles, Press Release, Eyewitness Accounts, etc.

Topics to Utilize Strategy: Unlimited.

Explanation: Reporting on an event, using a variety of sources. Excellent way to incorporate historical fiction writing, by writing mock interviews with "witnesses."

Topics to Utilize Strategy: Unlimited.

Historical Fiction

Definition: A literary work in which the characters are fiction, weaved into actual historical events.

Explanation: By combining a variety of strategies into this type, the student-writer has some freedom, and can better incorporate a historical message into their work.

Topics to Utilize Strategy: Unlimited.

Historical Reporting

Definition: To make known about the history of an event; intended for a news story.

Human-Interest Stories

Definition: A story relating to the personal experiences of those involved in historical actions. Personal life accounts.

Explanation: Historical fiction pieces on "witnesses" to history.

Topics to Utilize Strategy: Unlimited.

Humor Columns

Definition: A comical or whimsical look at historical events, presented with a series of articles.

Explanation: Satirical look at events of history. Can focus on specific events, movements, or people. Done in a manner to provide some humor, without being entirely critical.

Topics to Utilize Strategy: Unlimited.

I

Idioms

Definition: An expression having a meaning that cannot be understood from the individual meanings of its elements, as in *hand over fist*.

Explanation: Utilizing common American language traits to explain and relate methods of history. Two basic methods can be used with idioms. 1. Provide students with a list of idioms, and have them use them in a sentence that describes U.S. history. 2. Provide students with some historical events/people, and have them write idioms regarding the historical event/person. Examples of idioms can be found at any number of websites . . . search Idiom. Some examples are: "hair stand on end," "handwriting on the wall," and "face the music."

Topics to Utilize Strategy: Unlimited.

Images (see also Captions)

Definition: To describe especially vividly.

Explanation: Descriptive writing piece utilizing historical photographs, or historical settings. Display photos, and have students follow the guidelines below: 1. (PIP) person in picture, first person from the perspective of someone in photo. 2. Object in picture (OIP), first person from the perspective of an object in photo. 3. Person outside of picture (POP), witness to a photo. An interesting twist on this strategy is to require the students to research a photo, download it along with the source, and then do the writing assignment.

Topics to Utilize Strategy: Unlimited.

Imaginative Writings

Definition: Formation of a mental image that is not real or present.

Explanation: Ask students to describe a setting that they probably have never seen, or have limited access to. Example: Cold War Unit: Describe the inside of a missile room on a nuclear submarine.

Topics to Utilize Strategy: Unlimited in scope, but should be somewhat vague to students.

Impromptus

Definition: Done at the occasion, rather than being planned in advance.

Explanation: Opening activity to focus students toward a concept.

Prompt them, and ask them to write using various strategies . . . diary entry, ultimatums, antonyms/synonyms, cheers/chants, narrative, interior monologue, epitaphs, obituaries.

Topics to Utilize Strategy: Unlimited.

Instructions (similar to Directions)

Definition: A sequence of bits that tells a central process.

Explanation: This task is designed to allow students to look into details about the way in which things operate. Instructions should follow the specific process, and might require a research element.

Topics to Utilize Strategy: Military Weaponry, How to Load a Slave Ship, Paul Revere's Route, Passing of Bill into Law, Independence, MO to Oregon, Underground Railroad Route, Cotton Gin, Industrial Machinery, Stock Market and Why It Crashed, Guerilla Warfare, Bomb Shelter.

Interior Monologues

Definition: A speech by one person, specifically that which occurs while talking to one's self.

Explanation: Provides students an opportunity to relate first-hand accounts of important people. May be used as personification with events or movements.

Topics to Utilize Strategy: Presidents mulling over an important decision.

Interviews

Definition: A face-to-face conversation between two for the assessment of an applicant, or a conversation between a reporter and a subject.

Explanation: Emphasis can be place on dialogue writing. Great activity in a cross-curricular environment. Excellent opportunity for personification . . . . interviewing a place or object of importance; example: interviewing the cotton gin.

Topics to Utilize Strategy: Unlimited.

Introductions

Definition: To identify and present: to make strangers acquainted.

Explanation: Writing task in which students can write scripts that allow them to introduce people, places, or events from history. Can be used as a review activity in which students write introductions without providing the answer, and classmates guess the topic.

Topics to Utilize Strategy: Unlimited. Introductions can be made for people, places, years, decades, events, movements, cultural phenomenon's (dances, music, etc.).

Invitations

Definition: A request for someone's presence or attendance.

Explanation: Creative writing task allowing students to speculate on who would be present at specific events from history. May be altered to a hindsight activity in which people are invited to attend something they were present at (struggling Europe invites the U.S. soldiers before D-Day). Excellent opportunity for satire and irony to be implemented.

Topics to Utilize Strategy: New World to Explorers, Aztecs to Cortez, Plymouth to Pilgrims, Colonists to King George (Pleading), Native Americans to Custer, Oregon to Pioneers, West to Lewis & Clark, Slaves to Civil Rights, U.S. to Immigrants, Panama Canal to U.S., Depression to Roaring '20s, Great Migration Issues, Dallas to JFK, Vietnam to U.S.

J

Job Applications

Definition: The form in which a request is made for employment.

Explanation: Students design applications for specific people or tasks that have influenced history, and then answer the questions. Can be done as an exchange task in which one student designs the application and a different student answers the questions.

Topics to Utilize Strategy: Soldiers, Immigrants, Indentured Servants, Miners, Frontiersman, River Guides, Trappers, Secret Service, Hippies, Protestors.

Journals (see also Diaries)

Definition: A personal record of daily experiences and reflections; a diary.

Explanation: Students write from the perspective of a specific person in history, or take on the role of an event. This is an excellent opportunity for personification in student writing. Length suggestion: One paragraph up to a full paper (similar to autobiography, but focus can be on one day's events).

Topics to Utilize Strategy: Important People, Bystanders to a Situation (Witness to Boston Massacre, Witness on Grassy Knoll in Dallas), Objects of Historical Importance (Wagon Trains, Spinning Looms, Equipment Used in Panama, Statue of Liberty, U2 Spy Plane).

Junk Mail

Definition: Worthless or meaningless material passed through the mail.

Explanation: Creative writing opportunity that allows students to write about events of history that would be of no significance, or never came about. Examples could be advertisements for soldiers needed to fight WWIII. Allows for the use of propaganda and advertising techniques to be emphasized.

Topics to Utilize Strategy: Unlimited.

L

Leaflets

Definition: A printed handbill or flyer, sometimes written in a persuasive manner.

Explanation: Design a visual ad for making people aware of historical events, or opportunities they can participate in, persuasive in nature. To be used for billboards, news banners, or flyers.

Topics to Utilize Strategy: Colonization, Free Land in New World, Indentured Servants, Triangular Trade, Revolution, Minutemen Organizations, Ratification of Constitution, Land in Texas, Gold Rush, Underground Railroad, Land on Frontier, Political Machines, Soldiers for War,

Speakeasies, Stocks for Sale (Depression), Concentration Camps, Rosie Riveter, Bomb Shelter Sales, Rock & Roll Concerts, Great Society Programs, Montgomery Bus Boycott.

Lectures

Definition: A speech on a given subject delivered before an audience or class, as for the purpose of instruction.

Explanation: Students can become the teachers with this task writing up the content for a lecture. Similar in nature to an essay, but require students to include quotes, statistics, and facts for support. Done in a review fashion, students can lecture for 1-minute on various topics all related to a common theme.

Topics to Utilize Strategy: Unlimited.

Letters

Definition: A written or printed communication.

Explanation: Students are to write formal letters to historical figures, supporting, opposing, and questioning actions. This can also be assigned as a role-play letter in which the student takes on the role of a famous figure and writes a letter to a recipient.

Topics to Utilize Strategy: World Leader to World Leader, President to U.S. Citizen, President to War Hero, President to Family Member of Soldier, Citizen to Historical Figure, etc.

Letters to Editor

Definition: Written communication to newspaper editor for the purpose of disputing or agreeing with ideas expressed in the news service.

Explanation: Individual features providing students an opportunity to express opinions regarding a topic of history. May be implemented from historical perspective (Yes, that was a good/bad action), or writers take on the role of someone living during a historical event, and advise citizens or important people (similar to criticism).

Topics to Utilize Strategy: Unlimited . . . Is the World Flat?, Revolution Independence, Federalist vs. Anti-Federalist, Ratification, Secession, Manifest Destiny, Native American Perspective on Westward Expansion,

Labor Union Formation, Yellow Journalism, American Military Action ... Neutrality or War, Treaties, Atomic Bomb (Written to Truman), Berlin Airlift, Presidential Elections, Star Wars.

Lists

Definition: A series of names, words, or other items written or printed one after the other.

Explanation: A pre- or post-unit activity in which students brainstorm all thoughts regarding topics.

Topics to Utilize Strategy: Unlimited.

Logs (see Journals)

Definition: A regularly kept journal or record.

Topics to Utilize Strategy: See Journals.

M

Magazines

Definition: A periodical containing articles stories picture or other features.

Explanation: Similar to newspaper strategy. 1. Unit-ending project designed for class to complete. Assign individual members topics; assign an editor, and student work is combined to form a class magazine on a specific topic. 2. Semester project in which individual students complete a research based assignment on a topic or person of history (be cautious to avoid plagiarism with this type of task).

Topics to Utilize Strategy: Unlimited.

Manuals

Definition: A small reference book, usually providing instructions.

Explanation: This task is designed to allow students to look into details regarding the way in which things operate. Can be organized into a series of instructions. Instructions should follow the specific process and might require a research element.

Topics to Utilize Strategy: Military Weaponry, How to Load a Slave Ship, Paul Revere's Route, Passing of Bill into Law, Independence, Missouri to Oregon, Underground Railroad Route, Cotton Gin, Industrial Machinery, Stock Market and Why It Crashed, Guerilla Warfare, Bomb Shelter.

Maps

Definition: A representation, usually on a plane surface, of a region.

Explanation: This coincides with numerous types of strategies. One method is to ask students to answer a question regarding an event of history, and require a written answer that describes a map in the answer. Descriptions of maps require students to use detail in description. Maps can be provided or students can conduct research to locate a map.

Topics to Utilize Strategy: Unlimited.

Matchbook Covers

Definition: A brief note regarding a specific place or event, usually a type of advertisement, or satire regarding the topic. Found on matchbooks.

Explanation: Creative writing strategy offering a different approach.

Topics to Utilize Strategy: Unlimited.

Memoirs

Definition: An autobiography or biography.

Explanation: See autobiography or biography.

Topics to Utilize Strategy: Famous people or personification of events, inventions, movements, actions, or important elements of history (planes, cars, wagons, bombs, etc.).

Memory Writings (First Person)

Definition: First-hand accounts by persons involved in an activity.
Explanation: See journals or logs.
Topics to Utilize Strategy: Unlimited.

Messages and Memos

Definition: Short communication transmitted from one person or group to another.
Explanation: Students can put themselves in the place of a person, movement, or event from history and write a message from that perspective. Various strategies can be combined to make this strategy more focused.
Topics to Utilize Strategy: Unlimited.

Monologues

Definition: A long speech delivered by one person, sometimes containing soliloquy.
Explanation: First-person writing or personification of an event or movement. Similar to an interior monologue, only meant for an audience.
Topics to Utilize Strategy: Unlimited.

Movie Reviews

Definition: A written critique of a motion picture.
Explanation: Provide students with an opportunity to review a movie, and look at its historical value. Provide students with specific details to be followed in order to prevent plagiarism. (Completing a model in class prior to assignment is suggested to improve student comprehension.) Use caution with regard to plagiarism (requiring specific elements or a specific format will steer students away from copying from Internet).
Topics to Utilize Strategy: Unlimited.

Myths

Definition: A traditional ancient story dealing with supernatural beings or heroes that serve as a primordial type in the worldview of people.

Explanation: Creative writing task requiring students to explore the culture and legends of society.

Topics to Utilize Strategy: Unlimited.

N

Names

Definition: To mention, specify, or cite by name; to give a name to.

Explanation: Assignment similar to synonym strategy. Provide students with a list of events or people, and ask them to rename them. Works well as a review activity.

Topics to Utilize Strategy: Unlimited.

Narrations

Definition: To supply a descriptive commentary for a movie or performance.

Explanation: Script-writing task emphasizing use of language and personal thoughts.

Topics to Utilize Strategy: Unlimited.

Nature Studies

Definition: An inquiry or investigation of a natural setting.

Explanation: Writing task to emphasize the geographic setting of a historical era, movement or event. Utilization of other strategies can be focused towards the natural environment of a place. Example: poem about D-Day, advertisement for pioneers to come West, emphasizing the landscape and beauty of the Willamette Valley.

Topics to Utilize Strategy: Unlimited.

Newsletters

Definition: A printed report giving news or information or interest to a special group.

Explanation: Features on specific topics allow for students to take an in-depth look at areas of history. Such programs as *Microsoft Publisher* allow for students to implement the use of technology. Use extreme caution with regard to plagiarism.

Topics to Utilize Strategy: Unlimited.

Newspapers

Definition: A publication containing current news, editorials, feature articles, and advertising; usually published daily, weekly, or monthly.

Explanation: 1. Unit-ending project designed for class to complete. Assign individual members a topic; assign an editor, and student work is combined to form a class newspaper on a specific topic, or for a specific day, week, or month. 2. Semester project in which individual students complete a research-based assignment on a topic, or person of history. Be cautious to avoid plagiarism with this strategy.

Topics to Utilize Strategy: Unlimited.

News Stories

Definition: Individual story with a specific focus or topic meant for a publication.

Explanation: Can utilize historical fiction or nonfiction to write historically accurate news stories. Various strategies can be implemented for the news story. Combining several make a great newspaper activity. Implementation of a news story that makes predictions requires students to explore the cause/effect of an event or movement. *Example:* "Now that *Brown vs. Board* has been issued, what might happen in the U.S.?" Use caution with regard to plagiarism.

Topics to Utilize Strategy: Unlimited, but excellent as review activity.

Notes

Definition: A brief written record.

Explanation: 1. Students take on the role of a person that was part of a historical event and take notes regarding the situation. Teachers need to direct topics so that students have a general idea. 2. Provide a listening opportunity for students to take notes. Then have class exchange to emphasize, and discuss how to listen and take notes.

Topics to Utilize Strategy: Unlimited.

Notices (see Advertisements)

Definition: A written or printed announcement.

Topics to Utilize Strategy: Unlimited.

Novels

Definition: Fictional prose narrative of considerable length, typically having a plot.

Explanation: Extended writing opportunity usually for a semester or yearlong project.

Topics to Utilize Strategy: Unlimited.

Novelettes

Definition: A mini novel.

Explanation: Extended writing activity usually for a semester project activity.

Topics to Utilize Strategy: Unlimited.

O

Obituaries

Definition: A published notice of death usually with a brief biography of the deceased.

Explanation: Students are to write obituaries for historical figures, people, events, movements, decades, etc. Research the life and times of specific parts of history, and write it in a glorifying manner.

Topics to Utilize Strategy: Individual People (JFK), Eras (Progressive), Movements (Imperialism), Decades (Roaring '20s), Tribal Groups (Plains Indians), Wars (WWII), Events (Montgomery Bus Boycott).

Opinions

Definition: A belief or conclusion held with confidence but not substantiated by proof.

Explanation: Individual features providing students an opportunity to express opinions regarding a topic of history. They may be implemented from historical perspective (Yes, that was a good/bad action), or writers take on the role of someone living during a historical event, and advise citizens or important people (similar to criticism).

Topics to Utilize Strategy: Is the World Flat?, Revolution or Independence, Federalist vs. Anti-Federalist, Ratification, Secession, Manifest Destiny, Native American Perspective on Westward Expansion, Labor Union Formation, Yellow Journalism, American Military Action . . . Neutrality or War, Treaties, Atomic Bomb (Written to Truman), Berlin Airlift, Presidential Elections, Star Wars.

Ordinances

Definition: A municipal statute or communication.

Explanation: Students can write laws that would be applicable for time periods or events in history.

Topics to Utilize Strategy: Jim Crow Laws, Slave Guidelines on Plantations, Indentured Servant Rules, Wagon Train Chore Lists, Protest Movement Rules, Urban Laws for Immigrants.

P

Package Contents

Definition: Material contained in a specific parcel or object.

Explanation: Students can write the contents of a "delivery" that had a major impact on history. Can be a specific item, movement, or event. Contents should also include the potential effects that might result.

Topics to Utilize Strategy: Columbus's Ships, Indentured Servants, Wagon Trains, Slave Ship, Underground Railroad Escapees, Cotton Gin, Bombs, Immigrant Descriptions, Malaria Vaccine in Panama, Automobile Fresh off the Assembly Line, American Soldier to Normandy, Great Society Aid, Marshall Plan Care Package.

Pamphlets (see Brochures)

Definition: Unbound printed work with a paper cover, typically tri-fold.
Explanation:
Topics to Utilize Strategy: Unlimited.

Paragraphs

Definition: A brief article; distinct division of written or printed text.
Explanation: Short writing task to get students to understand the concept of framing a topic, specifically for a major paper.
Topics to Utilize Strategy: Unlimited.

Paraphrase

Definition: A restatement of a text or passage in another form or other words.
Explanation: Summary writing task to check for understanding. After reading a passage, students should paraphrase what they read. An excellent review activity. Supports development of reading skills. Can be altered so that paraphrase activity seeks to focus on specific facts or information.
Topics to Utilize Strategy: Unlimited . . . Textbook Passages, Primary Source Document, Poems, Famous Speeches.

Partisan Opinions

Definition: A one-sided opinion regarding a topic or issue. A belief or conclusion held with confidence but not substantiated by proof.
Explanation: Individual features providing students an opportunity to express opinions regarding a topic of history. May be implemented from

historical perspective (Yes, that was a good/bad action), or writers take on the role of someone living during a historical event, and advise citizens or important people (similar to criticism).

Topics to Utilize Strategy: Is the World Flat?, Revolution or Independence, Federalist vs. Anti-Federalist, Ratification, Secession, Manifest Destiny, Native American Perspective on Westward Expansion, Labor Union Formation, Yellow Journalism, American Military Action . . . Neutrality or War, Treaties, Atomic Bomb (Written to Truman), Berlin Airlift, Presidential Elections, Star Wars.

Patent Rights

Definition: A grant made by a government giving exclusive rights to the creator of an invention.

Explanation: Students write a description of a patent. This could be for an actual item or can be for an event or historical plan/legislation.

Topics to Utilize Strategy: Unlimited.

Personifications

Definition: To think of or represent an inanimate object as a person.

Explanation: Students write from the first-person perspective as they take on the role of an event, action, or movement of history. Excellent opportunity to utilize and combine strategies. Example: bio-poem for the Constitution, autobiography of a pony being used for Pony Express.

Topics to Utilize Strategy: Unlimited.

Persuasions

Definition: To induce or undertake a course of action, or to change someone's opinion through argument, reason, or entreaty.

Explanation: Writing task that requires students to voice opinions and influence in a positive manner. Usually done in the form of an essay, but may utilize other strategies. This is an excellent form of essay question for a test, providing students a creative option.

Topics to Utilize Strategy: Unlimited.

Petitions

Definition: A formal document containing a request or entreaty, usually meant for signatures.

Explanation: Encourage students to write the explanation of a petition that might have been circulated during a period of history. Usually focusing on events in which one group was unhappy with current life situation. Can be implemented with personification.

Topics to Utilize Strategy: Minuteman, Federalists, Slave Ships, Native Americans, 49ers, Slaves, Immigrants, Child Labor, Freedom Riders, Bombers, Doves/Hawks.

Philosophies

Definition: A system of values by which one lives.

Explanation: Strategy requiring the writer to research facts and transpose that into a clear understanding of topic. These can be people, places, events, or movements in history.

Topics to Utilize Strategy: Unlimited.

Photo Captions

Definition: A short description accompanying a picture.

Explanation: An excellent activity to challenge minds to think. Display photos on overhead or pass a series of photos around room, requiring each student to write an appropriate caption. After writing, have students read or listen to others, which provides a variety of ideas to be shared and absorbed by each student. This is an excellent opening or closing activity, which can be expanded into a task in which the students search for several photos, and write appropriate captions for each.

Topics to Utilize Strategy: Unlimited.

Picket Signs

Definition: Phrases on a placard carried by people that are expressing grievances or protesting.

Explanation: A creative implementation is to create picket signs for inanimate objects from historical events. (Bombers or Aircraft Carriers Go on Strike!)
Topics to Utilize Strategy: Unlimited.

Placards (see Plaques)

Definition: A sign or notice for public display; a nameplate on door.
Topics to Utilize Strategy: Unlimited.

Plaques

Definition: An engraved plate used for decoration or on a monument for information.
Explanation: Biographical type of writing activity similar to an obituary. Plaques can be done in a variety of strategies, and can have accompanying artwork or design.
Topics to Utilize Strategy: Unlimited: people, places, events, movements, and objects of influence.

Plays

Definition: A literary work for the stage.
Explanation: Students can duplicate events from history in one-act dramatizations that can be performed in front of the class, or utilized for a school-wide project and done as part of an assembly.
Topics to Utilize Strategy: Unlimited, but should be narrow in focus to highlight a specific event.

Playbills

Definition: A poster announcing a theatrical performance.
Explanation: Provide students with a title of a play and the basic plot. They then design and write copy for a playbill announcing the

performance. May be used in conjunction with the play-writing strategy. Actual plays can be used for this strategy.

Topics to Utilize Strategy: Unlimited.

Pledges

Definition: A formal promise; to promise to join.

Explanation: Students are to write a pledge for a group fighting for a cause. Use the United States' "Pledge of Allegiance" as a model.

Topics to Utilize Strategy: Unlimited.

Poems

Definition: A composition characterized by the use of condensed language, chosen for its sound and suggestive power.

Explanation: Providing students with poetic forms and style elements, this strategy allows students to utilize creative expression in their writing.

Topics to Utilize Strategy: Unlimited.

Point of Views (see Opinions)

Definition: A personal perspective regarding a conclusion held with confidence but not substantiated by proof.

Topics to Utilize Strategy: See Opinions.

Policies

Definition: A plan or course of action intended to influence and determine decisions, actions, and other matters.

Explanation: Students can rewrite history with this activity. Putting themselves in the role of president/policymaker, how would they have done it differently? An analytical approach to looking at history by exploring alternatives to events.

Topics to Utilize Strategy: Unlimited.

Preambles

Definition: A preliminary statement to a formal document, explaining its purpose.

Explanation: A type of summary for a reading assignment. Utilize the preamble to the U.S. Constitution as a model. After reading a selection, students are to write a preamble emphasizing the purpose and intent. Usually done with a formal piece of writing that was intended to make changes in history.

Topics to Utilize Strategy: Unlimited.

Predictions

Definition: To state, tell, or make known in advance.

Explanation: This strategy is designed for students to use what they already know (hindsight is 20/20), and write about how they think an event will change the future. Predicting the future and supporting it with historical facts. Another way in which to use this is to have students read presidential inaugural addresses, and then write a predictive story (JFK in 1960 is a good example).

Topics to Utilize Strategy: What Will Happen after Columbus's Successful Voyage, End of American Revolution, End of the Civil War, Analysis of Presidential Address, News Story about the Future of the World on September 1, 1945.

Press Conferences

Definition: An interview held for news reporters by a political figure or famous individual.

Explanation: Students become experts on a subject, and then write dialogue for a press conference about a major event in history. If they take on a personification role there is less chance of plagiarism. Use extreme caution with regard to plagiarism.

Topics to Utilize Strategy: Unlimited.

Press Releases

Definition: A statement issued or made public by a political figure, usually intended to inform members of the press.

Explanation: Students become experts on a subject, and then write a news release for a press conference about a major event in history. If they take on a personification role, there is less chance of plagiarism. Use caution with regard to plagiarism.

Topics to Utilize Strategy: Unlimited.

Profiles (see Biographies)

Definition: A brief biographical essay.

Topics to Utilize Strategy: See Biographies.

Prophecies (see Predictions)

Definition: To predict; foretell. To reveal by divine inspiration.

Topics to Utilize Strategy: Unlimited.

Q

Questions

Definition: An expression or inquiry that calls or asks for a reply.

Explanation: What type of questions would you ask a major "player" in history, and what would their potential answer be? This combines several strategies to achieve comprehension of a topic.

Topics to Utilize Strategy: Unlimited.

Questionnaires

Definition: A set of questions usually intended to gather information for a survey.

Explanation: Students take on the role of reporter as they develop questions for interviews. Time frame on this may be during a historical event or a type of assignment that students study those that lived through a historical event.

Topics to Utilize Strategy: Unlimited.

Quips

Definition: A clever, witty, often sarcastic remark.

Explanation: Creative task in which students utilize humor and sarcasm to make light of historical actions. May be done as first-person biographical roles, or as personification of events or objects.

Topics to Utilize Strategy: Unlimited.

R

Rain Checks

Definition: An assurance that an offer will be honored at a later date.

Explanation: Students can write a declaration guaranteeing later action in history. This is a retrospective task in which they know the outcome of history.

Topics to Utilize Strategy: If the World is Round, Exploration Will Happen, Europe Telling New World We Will Come to New World, Calvary Telling Native Americans They Will Return, U.S. Telling Panama They Will Come Back When Disease Is "Cured," U.S. Telling South Vietnam We Will Fight Communism.

Recommendations

Definition: To commend to another as worthy or desirable; endorse.

Explanation: Students express as first-person autobiographers the desired outcome or an event. Personification is an excellent mode for this strategy.

Topics to Utilize Strategy: Unlimited.

Renditions

Definition: A translation or interpretation of a work.

Explanation: Students write their own variation after reading a selection. Reading selections could be historical fiction, true accounts, or presidential addresses. Can be combined with another strategy. Example: A poem that summarized JFK's 1960 inaugural address. Write a news story explaining FDR's 1932 inaugural address.

Topics to Utilize Strategy: Unlimited.

Retrospect

Definition: A review or contemplation of things in the past.

Explanation: First-person writing opportunity, or personification piece. This is an excellent opportunity to combine strategies. Examples: Poems, Journal Entries, Monologues, and Interior Monologues.

Topics to Utilize Strategy: Unlimited.

Revisions

Definition: A modification or new edition of a work.

Explanation: After exploring a written element of history, students will then rewrite to include issues that should have been included, or if laws have changed, how have they been changed.

Topics to Utilize Strategy: Unlimited. Some examples to model with: Rewrite the preamble in common language. Rewrite passages of the Constitution addressing changes that have been made.

Riddles

Definition: A puzzling question or statement requiring thought to answer or understand.

Explanation: Students are to pick an event or person from history, and then write riddles using clues from their knowledge. An excellent method of review for unit or semester exams.

Topics to Utilize Strategy: Unlimited.

Road Signs

Definition: Descriptions found along roadways providing directions and marking points of reference.

Explanation: Creative task intended to highlight eras of history in which transportation has been expanded. *Road* may be substituted with *buoy, wagon train road, rail line,* or *Pony Express.* Excellent to use in conjunction with advertising and propaganda techniques.

Topics to Utilize Strategy: Unlimited.

Rules of Thumb

Definition: A useful principle having wide application but not intended to be strictly accurate.

Explanation: Students discuss the common practices of history, based upon events. A combination of creative elements or strategies can be implemented with this strategy.

Topics to Utilize Strategy: Unlimited.

Rumors

Definition: A report of uncertain origin and accuracy; hearsay.

Explanation: Creative writing task designed for students to explore all angles of an event, person, or movement. Emphasis should be placed on the speculative nature of society, especially in more recent decades.

Topics to Utilize Strategy: Unlimited.

S

Salutes

Definition: To honor formally.

Explanation: A formal written piece to honor a person or event. May be combined with a variety of strategies. Salutes may be in the form of poems, plaques, bumper stickers, commercials, idioms, journals, and playbills.

Topics to Utilize Strategy: Unlimited.

Sanctions

Definition: Authoritative permission or approval; a coercive measure adopted usually by several nations against a nation violating international laws.

Explanation: Written explanation for historical actions or events.

Topics to Utilize Strategy: Unlimited.

Sarcasms

Definition: A cutting, often ironic remark.

Explanation: Creative task in which students utilize humor and sarcasm to make light of historical actions. May be done as a first-person biographical role or as personification of events or objects.

Topics to Utilize Strategy: Unlimited.

Satires

Definition: A work in which human vice or folly is attacked through irony derision or wit; irony or caustic wit used to expose human folly.

Explanation: Creative task in which students utilize wit and irony and possibly sarcasm to make light of historical actions. May be done as a first-person biographical role, or as personification of events or objects.

Topics to Utilize Strategy: Unlimited.

Schedules

Definition: A list of items; a program of events or appointments; a timetable.

Explanation: Timeline activity in which students can reenact historical events with a retrospective angle. May incorporate art and design into the schedule.

Topics to Utilize Strategy: Unlimited.

Scripts (see News or Plays)

Definition: The text of a broadcast play or movie.
Topics to Utilize Strategy: See News or Plays.

Self-Images

Definition: A person's conception of one's self.
Explanation: Autobiographical sketch to be combined with a variety of strategies.
Topics to Utilize Strategy: Unlimited.

Serenades

Definition: A musical performance given to honor or express love or gratitude for someone.
Explanation: Writing task that implements music. A serenade may be combined with other strategies to make it more effective.
Topics to Utilize Strategy: Unlimited, but should focus on an event, movement, or person.

Short Stories

Definition: Short prose fiction with few characters aiming at unity or effect.
Explanation: Excellent method to implement historical fiction writing.
Topics to Utilize Strategy: Unlimited.

Skits (see Plays)

Definition: A short comical theatric sketch.
Topics to Utilize Strategy: Unlimited.

Slogans

Definition: A phrase expressing the aims or nature of an enterprise or group.

Explanation: Advertising activity that allows students to express positive attributes regarding participation in an event or movement.

Topics to Utilize Strategy: Presidential Candidates, Indentured Servants, Explorations, Wagon Trains, 49ers, Underground Railroad Ads, Soldiers to Enlist, Immigration, Suffrage, Bonus Army, Great Migration.

Soliloquy

Definition: A dramatic discourse in which a character reveals his or her own thoughts when alone or unaware of the presence of other characters.

Explanation: First-person writing task or personification task allowing students to speculate on people or events of history. Providing students with prompts is an excellent method to focus their writing.

Topics to Utilize Strategy: Unlimited . . . example: "On this bus, this day 12/5/1955, I could not believe what I saw . . . I saw the whites of their eyes, before the soldier holding me, but when he saw the whites, I erupted with a sharp rapport. . . . I was a musket about to help "Revolutionize America."

Songs

Definition: A brief composition written for singing.

Explanation: Creative writing task similar to a poem. Encourage students to use a familiar tune, and write new lyrics that represent the current topic being studied.

Topics to Utilize Strategy: Unlimited.

Sonnets

Definition: A 14-line poetic verse form usually in iambic pentameter, with a fixed rhyme pattern.

Explanation: Excellent to use in a cross-curricular setting. Provide students with examples of sonnets and allow them to substitute terms relevant to current studies.

Topics to Utilize Strategy: Unlimited.

Statue Plaques

Definition: An engraved plate used for decoration on a personal monument.

Explanation: Biographical type of writing activity similar to an obituary. Plaques can be done in a variety of strategies and can have accompanying artwork or design. Requiring students to write an inscription for a plaque or statue not already designed allows them to become the history writer.

Topics to Utilize Strategy: Unlimited: people, places, events, movements, and objects of influence.

Stereotypes

Definition: A conventional, oversimplified conception, opinion, or image.

Explanation: Short writing task asking students to explore how some groups are looked down upon in society. This poses a risk in offending students, so for privacy, emphasize no names on papers just to get lists to serve as discussion material.

Topics to Utilize Strategy: Unlimited.

Strategies

Definition: A plan of action.

Explanation: What is your plan? Ask students to write a plan of action for an event. This will allow them to look at history, and write fact-based strategies. They can include strategies they know were ineffective, but have altered with the benefit of retrospect.

Topics to Utilize Strategy: War plans, movement plans, event planning.

Subpoenas

Definition: A writ requiring appearance in court to give testimony.

Explanation: Modify the subpoena to require someone or some event to show up and give testimony. Who would students request attend a discovery hearing regarding a historical event?

Topics to Utilize Strategy: Unlimited.

Summations

Definition: A concluding statement summarizing the principle points.
Explanation: Summary of reading selections.
Topics to Utilize Strategy: Unlimited

Surveys (see Questionnaire)

Definition: A detailed investigation or inspection.
Topics to Utilize Strategy: Unlimited.

Synonyms

Definition: A word having the same or nearly the same meaning as another word in a language.
Explanation: Allows students to use adjectives and adverbs to describe specific events in history. Utilized like a Rorschach ink blot test. Teacher provides a list of events (orally or written); students provide synonyms for the event. May also be done with antonyms. This works well as a semester review activity.
Topics to Utilize Strategy: Unlimited.

T

Telegrams

Definition: A communication that is sent through coded signals; usually grammatically incorrect, focusing on the highlights of the content.
Explanation: Newsflash! A quick writing task for students to state the important facts. Implementation of this while studying historical eras in which telegrams were the most important form of communication emphasizes the content and the development of communication techniques.

Topics to Utilize Strategy: Unlimited, but should focus on major events. "GLD FND . . . PRL BMBD, GRMNY QTS."

Testimonies

Definition: A declaration by witness under oath; a public declaration.
Explanation: Personification opportunity in which objects are questioned about events.
Topics to Utilize Strategy: Unlimited.

Timelines (see Calendars)

Definition: A representation of key events in a specific time period.
Topics to Utilize Strategy: Unlimited.

U, V, W

Ultimatums

Definition: A statement of terms that expresses or implies the threat of serious penalties if the terms are not accepted.
Explanation: A preview of what is to come . . . with the benefit of retrospective knowledge.
Topics to Utilize Strategy: Unlimited.

Vanity Plates

Definition: A specific word or code phrase on a license plate representing the owner of the vehicle.
Explanation: Creative writing opportunity to design plates for people, places, or events.
Topics to Utilize Strategy: Unlimited.

Warranties

Definition: A legally binding guarantee.

Explanation: A guarantee that future action will take place. Similar to a prediction. This can be done with a retrospective angle in which students "predict" what will happen based upon actual events.

Topics to Utilize Strategy: Unlimited.

Welcomes

Definition: Greet, receive, or accept with pleasure; written statement of such.

Explanation: Writing strategy for students to speculate on how newcomers to an area or event would be welcomed. This can be done in a positive light (Americans entering concentration camps) or a negative light (Aztecs to Cortez).

Topics to Utilize Strategy: Unlimited.

Wills

Definition: A legal declaration of how a person wishes his or her possessions be disposed of after death.

Explanation: A creative method to this strategy is to write wills for events, movements, and cultures. This allows for more than just people to be explored.

Topics to Utilize Strategy: Unlimited, but should focus on someone or event that "lost out" in history.

Witticisms

Definition: A clever or humorous remark or answer.

Explanation: Creative task in which students utilize humor and sarcasm to make light of historical actions. May be done as first-person biographical roles, or as personification of events or objects.

Topics to Utilize Strategy: Unlimited.

5

Student Examples

The following provide examples of writing samples completed by students in an eleventh grade U.S. history class.

PERSUASIVE ESSAY/EDITORIAL/MONOLOGUE

The sons of liberty want you to join us and retaliate against the lobster backs!! Do you want to wake up every morning knowing that people in our colony are eating tea and crumpets for breakfast? Do you want to improve our dentistry because teeth really are that important? Who wants to live in a colony that is still ruled by tyrannical kings and queens anymore? And finally, who wants to be taxed on things like tea, stamps, and sugar? It is outrage, and they will not stop unless we force them into submission! We must fight!

Do we want our colonies ruled by people who invent anti-colonist acts such as the Sugar Act? The only reason that they put a new tax on foreign-made molasses is so they can get out of debt from the war. The sugar act will reduce our merchant's profits, and those who are accused of violating the act will be tried in a vice-admiralty court with one judge instead of sympathetic colonialists. We must fight!

The British also invented the Stamp Act! Do you remember being outraged from the taxes on printing newspaper, documents, etc.? We have! We boycotted, yes we know, and it worked, but the British invented another act right after the Stamp Act. This proves that smelly Englishmen are non-merciful with their inventing of acts. We must fight!

On March 5, 1770, some of our loyal colonists were merely standing in front of the Boston Customs house when those red coats fired shots at us! Five of our best men were killed, murdered, and massacred. We cannot go down in history as being ruled by people who have ugly British wives, and bad food! We must fight!

The British put a tax on tea. TEA!!!! Come on Brits, I expected more from you, and it's not like we can't drink coffee with our scones and crackers. We don't want your tea and we don't want your taxes! In fact we might just dress up as Indians and feed your tea to the fishes. Taxing us so you can save your own company, the bankrupt British East India Company. It is pathetic, and we must fight!

As you can see, the British are ruthless, selfish, and ill-tempered. They will keep taxing us, and creating new acts to try and take our money, but we know better now. If we merely protest, we will be massacred. We must devise a plan, a war tactic, and a rebellion against the lobster backs! Your colony needs YOU to help us rebel against the British and have a nation of our own! WE MUST FIGHT! We must kill the British before they tax all our money away so we cannot buy weapons! We must rid the Brits from our land now. We must Fight!

PROFILE/BIOGRAPHY

The Delaware River as we know it today was named the South River by the Dutch for being the main highway through the southern part of the New Netherland colony. Along with Manhattan Island in New York, the river supported one of the few hubs of multiculturalism in the early American colonies. The settlers were a mixture of Dutch, English, Swedes, Finns, Germans, and others. The state of Delaware partly owes its existence to the short-lived Dutch settlement of Swaanendael that depended on this river daily. The river lies between the states of Delaware, New Jersey, and Pennsylvania. It is navigable by large, oceangoing vessels as far inland as Philadelphia and by smaller vessels to Trenton, New Jersey. The Chesapeake and Delaware Canal connects the Delaware River below Wilmington, Delaware, with Chesapeake Bay. From George Washington's crossing during one revolution, to the birthplace of America's next revolution, to a the Civil War, and finally to a World War, it seems as though the Delaware River has been at the center of United States history.

One of the river's most famous duties came on the evening of December 25, 1776, when George Washington led his troops across the Delaware. Using the cover of what would soon be night they moved across the calm Delaware. He had planned on surprising the English and Hessian troops in the Battle of Trenton the day after Christmas. The next day was a decisive victory over the British Crown and her mercenaries. It marked a turning point in the Revolutionary War and in United States history.

The Delaware River passes by Pennsylvania's Lehigh Valley, birthplace of another revolution known as America's Industrial Revolution. Before the early twentieth century all sources of power came from animal or water. Factories in the nineteenth century relied heavily on water for power. It is for this reason that America's Industrial Revolution would begin near a major waterway. The large cities of the North fueled the boom of factories that were built during this time.

During the Civil War Confederate Soldiers were imprisoned on an island of the river. At the mouth of the New Castle River was Pea Patch Island. Nearly 12,000 Confederate soldiers were imprisoned on Pea Patch Island during the Civil War. The Delaware River protected Pea Patch Island from attacks by land. Strategically, a military facility would not be built where it was vulnerable. Clearly, the river island was a safe place to keep prisoners of war.

In 1915, the United States saw the need for a shipyard on the Delaware River. To meet the intense war demand, the world's largest shipyard at the time was built along the Delaware. This massive shipyard was built on Hog Island, offshore of Philadelphia. Prior to the shipyard's construction, United States' cargo boats had been sunk by German U-boats. To combat these attacks the United States needed a large shipyard. The Delaware River was clearly chosen again for its size and stable waters.

In conclusion, from Washington's crossing in 1776, to the birth-place of America's next revolution, to the Civil War in the 1860's, and finally to the United States' involvement in a World War in 1917, it seems as though the Delaware River has been at the center of United States history. The Delaware has protected and nurtured countless events and wars throughout the United States of America's history. The river's stable waters and size has kept it constantly in the spotlight.

FREE WRITE/COMPARISON

The American Dream

The American dream is what all people living in the United States strive to achieve. Each and every person has a different idea of what this dream is, while still keeping their minds set on one general idea. This idea consists of being the best off and the happiest that any person or family could be. The American dream used to consist of want-ing a white picket fence in the front yard, being healthy, wealthy, and happy. The American dream also consisted of a safe nation where the youth of each generation could live in a safe and fearless nation with the guarantee that nothing in the way of a huge war like the civil war or WWII would ever happen while they still lived. While that has never changed with time, the other parts of the dream have with coming generations.

Nowaday's people's American dream consists mainly of money, money, and more money (greed). To the youth of today, money is what makes the world go round. Without it nothing can be achieved and its due mostly in part to the new technology produced everyday. Nowadays because of items like TV, video games, and computers (technology) people are less intelligent and more overweight than they should be because these types of things make people lazy and not want to exercise like they should, in turn make many unhealthy. Without much of this technological crap, the United States' American dream would be much more focused on what's better for us all as a whole rather than just one person!

CRITICISM

Topic: Louisiana Purchase

Just what were we thinking when we did this? The Louisiana Purchase could turn out to be one of the biggest mistakes of this administration. What makes this vast expanse of wild land worth 12 million dollars? Why should we trust a man that is trying to take over Europe? For all we know he will use the 12 million and try to catch the United States by surprise with an attack and try to add us to his empire. Yes, sooner or later we must expand to accommodate our growing population, but buying all this land will necessitate a need to defend it, and we will meet fierce resistance from the Indians. This purchase will create many conflicts with both them and Mexico. And, with the increased conflicts, comes a greater chance to start another war, and I think we have had enough of those. This land contains many resources, but do we have the population to man the factories and do all the work necessary to harvest such an abundant land? All things considered, I feel this purchase is no more than President Jefferson overstepping the boundaries of the office he holds.

PERSONIFICATION

The Mississippi River's View of the Louisiana Purchase

Being the Mississippi River is not any easy job as many would assume. Most think that being a river would be simple, just flowing from here to there. But now that the Louisiana Territory has been purchased by President Thomas Jefferson and his Secretary of State James Monroe, I fear that my work load may increase. I think that since America now has the advantage of my services, I can provide for them more than anything they've ever had before. I can offer them the ability to send ships carrying goods from the mid-west down my swift waterway, out into the ocean, giving the opportunity for them to trade goods to other countries of the world. This could possibly make America one of the most profitable and lucrative countries in the world, letting them build an empire. France's use of my abilities were great, no doubting that, but I believe that America's will be even greater. My rationale behind this is that America is so much closer to me than France is, allowing them to use me more frequently. So with that I am very excited about my new owner and I look forward to the new work load. As they say, France's loss is America's gain.

HEADLINES

Examples from the 1950s

Black Man vs. White World: Robinson to Play in Big Leagues
Robinson Goes BIG!
Hello Mr. Fast Food: McDonald's Opens
How Fast Can Fast Food Be?
Storks Working OT: Baby's Everywhere
Checkers or Chess? (Election of '52)
U.S. to the Rescue Again (Marshall Plan Aid)
USSR Gets Hungary!

INTERVIEW/INTERIOR MONOLOGUE

The button was slowly depressed and the bull whir of the magnetic tape running through the recording mechanism began to move.

"So tell me why you're here, why has President Johnson sent you to fight?" There was a prolonged silence as I contemplated what the East Coast reporter had asked. Thoughts raced through my head. Why had we come to this desolate place? Why were we helping the French fight a bloody battle with Vietnam? Who was this enemy, Vietnam? I sat up in my bed and leaned against the rough canvas of the Mobile Army Surgery Hospital's post-operation tent.

"I think that it had a lot to do with Johnson's idea of containment of Communism, Johnson believes that if we defeat them on their own soil we can stop, or at least hinder the progress that they made thus far, around the world." This was a true statement, I thought, but is this what Kennedy would have done?

The reporter switched tactics, he started going for the more personal information. "What have you yourself given to this war?" he asked.

I don't think he was prepared for my answer. I slowly removed the wool sheets from my legs, or should I say, what is left of my legs. The reporter recoiled in disgust. The scarred fleshy stumps were destroyed tissue and bone from my lower legs. "That's what an Army of the Republic of Vietnam, or ARVN, land mine will do to the legs of U.S. soldiers." I continued to explain to this reporter. He asked what happened to the rest of my body. From my head to toe I was covered in deep third degree burns, grave wounds that had burned so profoundly that the flesh and nerves were utterly destroyed. I told him of the napalm that had been dropped on my position moments after I stepped on the mine. The napalm was extremely effective for scorching the earth and decimated the ranks of the soldiers, both Vietnamese and U.S.

The reporter was uncomfortable I could tell, and the interview was over before I could inform him of the foliage killing, Agent Orange, and the Search and Destroy missions where soldiers went into villages and killed the livestock, burned the crops, and murdered the innocent Vietnamese civilians. Even though I didn't get my entire message out, I believe I made my point about the U.S. involvement, and President Johnson's lies about the war.

PROPAGANDA

Topic: USSR Government Statement Regarding the Marshall Plan

The United States provided aid to sixteen different countries containing $13 billion in European nations, yet did not attempt to relieve the USSR whatsoever. This action of the United States demonstrates a great deal about money out to certain countries however unfairly don't provide to all. This act was deliberately directed toward the USSR as a threat and an attempt to show their improvement of image, but indirectly down grading the USSR, which only hindered the nation's appeal. The Americans' actions in the Marshall Plan prove their unequal ideas, which relates to their government that only can lead to corruption. The enemy's goal to have freedom will only cause chaos and destruction among society and could potentially lead to World War III. Who wants to go through that experience again? Utilizing wealth is exactly what the U.S. is doing to lure other countries into the idea of self-determination to stray from communism, which will create an imbalanced civilization. Since America sees the USSR as a threat and the well-accomplished idea of communism their goal is to destroy us. What human would want to end up like horrific destruction of Germany? The power of the United States must be countered and contained immediately, before it is too late and they take over the USSR and the entire world.

LETTER

Dear Mom & Dad,

I sure do appreciate your letters. It keeps me going to hear from you guys. It was miserably hot today, over 90 degrees. And the humidity is unbearable. We had to go on a Search and Destroy mission again today through the deadly jungle. Once again our goal was to find Vietcong tunnels. It is suspenseful because you never know where Charlie is hiding. Even if we don't find any VC, it is never easy going. The mosquitoes eat you alive, and what they don't get, the elephant grass does. One guy, Johnny is his name, got cut pretty bad, and we had to bandage him up.

Man, I hate it here. Everything we do seems pointless. I sure hope Westmoreland and Johnson know what they are doing. But don't worry, I'm managing, and the best part, I get to come home in 93 days. Believe me, I am counting everyone!

We heard that Johnson might send more troops here. That would be nice. We seem outnumbered each time we go on patrol. You wouldn't believe the tunnels the VC have dug. All the secret passages and booby traps make it nearly impossible to have any success. I guess it is success, taking out a VC village. The air raids don't seem to do any good either, with the enemy always underground.

The food here is horrible, nothing like your cooking mom. I can't wait to get home to one of your home cooked meals. Say hi to everyone for me. I sure miss you guys. Oh yeah, please write more, and send a care package if you get a chance. The guys look forward to anything from the good old USA.

Your son, Jack

NEWS STORY/PREDICTION

It has been one month since the violence in the Pacific has ended; one month since the awesome and destructive power of the atomic bomb has been revealed to Americans, and the rest of humanity. This single act, which had ended one of the greatest wars of all time, has also succeeded in ending the idea of a nuclear free world. Although our soldiers are gaining help from the GI Bill of Rights, and America will probably soon experience a tremendous baby boom, the future does not look so bright. In sight of this stunning knowledge of atomic destruction, we must prepare for what is yet to come.

Where does the next threat against democracy loom, red China? Perhaps Korea? What part of the world will the U.S.S.R reach out towards next?

The lust for conquest will begin with a massive arms race, to see which nation can out do the other in destructive and powerful weaponry. These new ways to induce death will be unimaginable, and will begin to affect the way we live our lives. Soon, nonetheless, these nations will find that weaponry is not enough to win this silent war. They will begin to look upward at the stars and another race to begin, a race into space. Massive planes will orbit the earth and spy from the heavens. However, amidst the chaos, confusion, and threat of a third world war, peace will still linger. Blocks of nations will be put together in order to stop the threat of bloodshed, and cut off the head of the viper before it has a chance to strike. This so-called peace however, will not to be able to resolve all conflicts and could eventually crumble.

About the Author

Scott Whipple is the social science department coordinator and classroom teacher at West Salem High School, in Salem, OR. He especially takes pride in the way in which his students experience history through active reading and writing activities that promote literacy development. Scott also serves as West Salem High School's representative to the Salem-Keizer school district Literacy Committee. In this role, he provides staff training and inservice seminars focused toward the promotion of school-wide literacy. Mr. Whipple has conducted staff development workshops in several areas including, writing across the curriculum, reading across the curriculum, alternative assessment, and speaking work samples in the content area classroom. In addition, he is a certified trainer for the Oregon Department of Education, focusing on the Social Science Analysis Work Sample. He has been a workshop presenter at the Oregon Department of Education's annual conference on literacy, the Oregon Council for Social Science Teachers annual conference, and the Salem-Keizer School District No Teacher Left Behind institute. Scott lives in Salem, OR with his wife of 14 years, Taffy, and their three children; Hannah Blayke (9), Paige Brooklyn (7), and Holden Trey (3). Active in athletics at the schools he has taught at and now with youth leagues, Scott enjoys coaching, focusing mostly on his children's teams. Hobbies include hiking and fishing, especially opportunities that take him back to his roots of North Douglas County and the Umpqua Valley.